Joint Workshop on NLP for Computer Assisted Language Learning and NLP for Language Acquisition 2016

Umea, Sweden
16 November 2016

Editors:

Elena Volodina
Gintare Grigonyte
Ildiko Pilan

Kristina Nilsson Bjorkenstam
Lars Borin

ISBN: 978-1-5108-3789-8

Proceedings of the joint workshop on NLP for Computer Assisted Language Learning and NLP for Language Acquisition

Preface
Elena Volodina, Gintarė Grigonytė, Ildikó Pilán,
Kristina Nilsson Björkenstam and Lars Borin

Conference description

The joint workshop on Natural Language Processing (NLP) for Computer-Assisted Language Learning (CALL) & NLP for Language Acquisition (LA) – shorthand NLP4CALL&LA – is an effort to provide a debate space and collaboration between two closely related areas. Both focus on language acquisition, related resources and technologies, that can support research of the language learning process as well as aim to bring interdisciplinary advantage to the field. Individual workshop areas are outlined below.

The area of NLP4CALL is applied in essence, where tools, algorithms, and ready-to-use programs play an important role. It has a traditional focus on *second* or *foreign* language learning, and the target age group of school children or older. The intersection of Natural Language Processing and Speech Technology, with Computer-Assisted Language Learning (CALL) brings "understanding" of language to CALL tools, thus making CALL intelligent. This fact has provided the name for this area of research – Intelligent CALL, ICALL. As the definition suggests, apart from having excellent knowledge of Natural Language Processing and/or Speech Technology, ICALL researchers need good insights into second language acquisition (SLA) theories and practices, second language assessment, as well as knowledge of L2 pedagogy and didactics.

The workshop on Language Processing for Research in Language Acquisition (NLP4LA) broadens the scope of the joint workshop to also include theoretical, empirical, and experimental investigation of first, second and bilingual language acquisition. NLP4LA aims to foster collaboration between the NLP, linguistics, psychology and cognitive science communities. The workshop is targeted at anyone interested in the relevance of computational techniques for first, second and bilingual language acquisition.

The joint workshop series on NLP4CALL&LA has arisen in 2016 and has become a meeting place for researchers working on the integration of Natural Language Processing and Speech Technologies in systems supporting language learning and research around it, and exploring the theoretical and methodological issues arising during language acquisition.

Motivation

Results of the Survey of Adult Competencies (PIAAC, 2013), where literacy as a skill has been assessed among the adult population (16–65 years) has shown that on average Sweden scored among the top 5 countries out of the 23 OECD participants. However, the national Swedish report quotes the difference between the average literacy levels of

Elena Volodina, Gintarė Grigonytė, Ildikó Pilán, Kristina Nilsson Björkenstam and Lars Borin 2016. Preface.
Proceedings of the joint workshop on NLP for Computer Assisted Language Learning and NLP for Language Acquisition at SLTC 2016. Linköping Electronic Conference Proceedings 130: i–viii.

native (L1) born citizens compared to citizens with an immigrant (L2) background as the largest observed among all participating countries (OECD, 2013:6). The low literacy population in Sweden has three times higher risk of being unemployed or reporting poor health. The survey results point to an acute need of supporting immigrants and other low-literacy groups in building stronger language skills as a way of getting jobs and improving lifestyle (SCB, 2013:8).

Besides, in the setting of an escalating refugee crisis in Europe and a growing number of people seeking asylum in Sweden (Migrationsverket 2016), research supporting second language acquisition, assessment and teaching is in every way important to the Swedish society. The government has recently initiated a project on learning among newly arrived (Skolverket 2014) where one of the foci is on producing tools for evaluation of Swedish as a second language, an aim to which the NLP4CALL workshop series contributes in a most robust way through bringing together people capable of influencig the situation through intelligent solutions. Exchange of information, ideas, experiences, methods, etc. between researchers dealing with ICALL questions leads to new insights and as a result to progress in the field.

In the recent debates, the Swedish government have been strongly encouraging immigrants to take a "fast path" to learn Swedish so that immigrants can be sooner considered for work in Sweden. However, the fast path is not a solution, according to SLA researchers[1] (Josefsson 2016). Professor Gunlög Josefsson in her article argues that the two immediate investments for improving teaching of L2 Swedish should be:

1. Development of effective IT-based solutions that can be used anywhere despite presence of a teacher

2. Education of a larger number of second language teachers that can offer SFI (Swedish For Immigrants) and other types of courses to greater number of immigrants,especially to those planning to take Swedish university courses as a step to validate their education.

The research outlined for this workshop targets directly the first point on Josefsson's agenda and indirectly supports the second point on the Josefsson's agenda. Language technologies can be used to create more effective tools and computerized solutions for online teaching of target languages; as well as to support and relieve teachers of tedious tasks that can be modelled, such as exercise generation, essay grading, etc. Most importantly, use of Language Technologies can make IT solutions for language learning more "intelligent".

Through this workshop, we intend to profile ICALL and LA research in the Nordic countries and to provide a dissemination venue for researchers active in this area.

The broad motivation of NLP4CALL & NLP4LA workshop is to provide a meeting place for researchers working on language learning issues including both empirical and experimental studies and NLP-based applications and to bring together competences from these areas for sharing experiences and brainstorming the future of the field.

---

1 <http://www.svd.se/professor-snabbspar-till-svenska-fungerar-inte/om/debatt>

Research background

Intelligent tools for language learning are within reach given the availability of key components: corpora, lexicons, tokenizers, lemmatizers, morphological analyzers, parsers, etc. (Nerbonne & Smit, 1996; Tufis, 1996). ICALL applications are based on (language-specific) tools that are used to process language samples (text, speech, words, etc.) and that have generative power of applying the same analysis model to different language samples over and over again, being an infinite source of language "wisdom" (e.g. automatic error correction, automatic exercise generation, etc). Depending upon the aim of an ICALL application the above-named key software can be assembled in various ways making use of their different features, thus facilitating diverse learning aims. Nowadays various ICALL applications can support reading and writing activities (Heilman et al., 2006; Mitkov & Ha, 2003), vocabulary (Volodina et al., 2014a), grammar (Meurers et al., 2010; Reynolds et al., 2014) as well as pronunciation and listening skills (Wik & Hjalmarsson, 2007). However, very often these efforts remain prototypes not leading to fully-functional systems that can be incorporated into educational establishments.

To successfully build a full-ended ICALL system, a wide spectrum of issues need to be addressed and solved:

* collection and annotation of learner-specific data, such as learner-specific lexicons, grammar profiles, annotated essays, reading comprehension corpora, etc.

* incorporation of the results of (S)LA research to gain appropriate linguistic features in combination with pedagogically relevant criteria to base automatic evaluation/ assessment on

* algorithms, methods, heuristic rules, etc. for data handling

* evaluation of tools, algorithms and programs with teachers and learners

* modeling of learners and learner progress for indivisualized learning

* feedback generation for encouraging progress on the learner side

As long as these areas are treated separately, a vision of a full-ended system remains utopian. However, without having each of the outlined issues solved/researched, there is no hope for making utopia a reality. That is why it is important to create a network of researchers working on various tasks within ICALL so that solutions prompted by them could be tested in other projects. The workshop creates a meeting space for sharing insights into the ICALL problems, uniting efforts and creating a network of experts in the field.

This workshop series covers all Language Acquisition-relevant research areas as outlined above, including studies where NLP-enriched tools are used for testing (S)LA and pedagogical theories, and vice versa, where (S)LA theories/pedagogical practices are modeled in hands-on tools.

This year our focus has been on how to tranfser from small individual research projects to a full-scale application ready for use in educational establishments: What needs to be done yet? Which approach is the most effective? What time estimation is realistic? Do we have enough expertise? Which collaboration do we need to establish? How? Do we lack manpower or financial support? Or both?

The two invited speakers presented ICALL from two points of view: commercial and academic.

The first invited speaker, **Jill Burstein**, is a Research Director of the Natural Language Processing Group in Research & Development at Educational Testing Service in Princeton, New Jersey[2]. Her research interests span Natural Language Processing for educational technology, automated essay scoring and evaluation, discourse and sentiment analysis, argumentation mining, education policy, English language learning, and writing research. The intersection of her interests has led to two extensively used commercial applications for English L2 learners: E-rater®, ETS' automated essay evaluation application, and the *Language Muse Activity Palette*^{TM} -- a new classroom tool under development targeting English learners that automatically generates language activities for classroom texts to support content comprehension. Jill Burstein is one of the most successful researchers within ICALL that together with a group of bright researchers made ICALL tools a reality for many teachers of L2 English. Her expertise and experience will be a highlight of the workshop.

The second invited speaker, **Piet Desmet,** is Full Professor of French and Applied linguistics and Computer-Assisted Language Learning at KU Leuven and KU Leuven KULAK. He coordinates the imec-research team ITEC (Interactive Technologies), focusing on domain-specific educational technology with a main interest in language learning & technology. He leads a range of research projects in this field focusing on such topics as adaptive and personalized learning, input enhancement, intelligent feedback or automated analysis and annotation of text corpora using natural language processing. He also coordinates the large-scale research project TECOL focusing on technology-enhanced collaborative learning. He is director of more than 15 PhDs (finished and ongoing) and author of publications in journals such as Language Learning & Technology, System, ReCALL or CALL Journal). He has been presenter at many international conferences (CALICO, WORLDCALL, EUROCALL, UNTELE, EDMEDIA, etc.) and organizer of different international symposia. He was involved in the creation of two spin-offs in the field. All this makes him a renowned scholar in our field with theoretical as well as practical contributions to the integration of NLP into CALL.

The two speakers represented two different worlds - the first one of a commercial company and the second one of an academic university. As practice shows, most tools, solutions and technologies developed at a university remain prototypical whereas commercial companies tend to take such solutions to the users. However, the two worlds are dependent on each other. Both invited speakers represented projects that over time have grown from small-scale initiatives to become influential trend-setting

---

2   The text is copied from <http://jillburstein.com/>

intelligent solutions in language learning.

Previous NLP4CALL workshops

The first five editions of this workshop series[3] have attracted participants from all over the world, including researchers from Australia, Canada, Central, South and Northern Europe, Russia as well as USA. The workshops have shown the vast potential that Language Technology (LT) holds for language learning and – most importantly – the interest that LT researchers have in the domain of CALL.

Previous workshop editions have covered numerous topics that can be grouped towards

- research directly aimed at ICALL, such as the analysis of learner-produced texts and the generation of L2 learning materials
- practices demonstrating actual or potential use of existing Speech Technologies, NLP tools or resources for language learning, such as automatic essay grading or using speech synthesis in spelling exercises
- research aimed at development of resources and tools with potential usage in ICALL, either directly in interactive applications, or indirectly in materials, application or curriculum development, e.g. collecting and annotating ICALL-relevant corpora; developing tools and algorithms for readability analysis, selecting optimal corpus examples, etc.
- discussion of challenges, visions and research agenda for ICALL

The special focus has always been given to discussion of the above-mentioned themes for the Nordic languages.

Submissions to the four workshop editions have targeted a wide variety of languages, ranging from well-resourced languages (German, English, French, Russian, Spanish) to under-resourced ones (Estonian, Saami, Võro), among which several Nordic languages have been targeted: Danish, Estonian, Icelandic, Norwegian, Saami, Swedish, and Võro.

Up to date, acceptance rate varied between 50% and 77% (Table 1), the average being 66,5%. The acceptance rate is rather high, however, the reviewing process has always been very strict with two-three double reviews per submission. This indicates that submissions to the workshops have always been of high quality.

Workshop year	Submitted	Accepted	Acceptance rate
2012	12	8	67%
2013	8	4	50%
2014	13	10	77%
2015	9	6	67%
2016	14	10	71,5%

Table 1. Submmissions and submission rates, 2012-2016

---

3 <http://www.spraakbanken.gu.se/icall>

Our many thanks go to our program committee consisting of internationally acknowledged researchers from many countries and continents representing different competences within ICALL and LA areas:

- Lars Ahrenberg, Linköping University, Sweden
- Florencia Alam, CONICET, Argentina
- Christina Bergmann, Centre National de la Recherche Scientifique, France
- Eckhard Bick, University of Southern Denmark, Denmark
- Lars Borin, University of Gothenburg, Sweden
- Antonio Branco, University of Lisboa, Portugal
- Jill Burstein, Educational Testing Service, USA
- Alex Cristia, Centre National de la Recherche Scientifique, ENS-DEC, EHESS, France
- Piet Desmet, KU Leuven Kulak, Belgium
- Simon Dobnik, University of Gothenburg, Sweden
- Thomas Francois, UCLouvain, Belgium
- Gintare Grigonyte, Stockholm University, Sweden
- Anna Gudmundsson, Stockholm University, Sweden
- Jana Götze, KTH, Sweden
- Björn Hammarberg, Stockholm University, Sweden
- Katarina Heimann Mühlenbock, DART, Sahlgrenska Universitetssjukhuset, Sweden
- Sofie Johansson Kokkinakis, University of Gothenburg, Sweden
- Chigusa Kurumada, University of Rochester, USA
- Peter Ljunglöf, Chalmers Tekniska Högskolan, Sweden
- Staffan Larsson, University of Gothenburg, Sweden
- Montse Maritxalar, University of the Basque country, Spain
- Ellen Marklund, Stockholm University, Sweden
- Detmar Meurers, University of Tübingen, Germany
- Kristina Nilsson Björkenstam, Stockholm University, Sweden
- John K. Pate, The University at Buffalo, USA
- Martí Quixal, University of Tübingen, Germany
- Lena Renner, Stockholm University, Sweden
- Gerold Schneider, University of Konstanz, Germany
- Mathias Schulze, University of Waterloo, Canada
- Iris-Corinna Schwarz , Stockholm University
- Philip Shaw, Stockholm University, Sweden
- Jennifer Spenader, University of Groningen, Netherlands
- Sofia Strömbergsson, Karolinska Institutet, Sweden
- Joel Tetreault, Yahoo! Labs, USA
- Trond Trosterud, Universitetet i Tromsø, Norway

- Cornelia Tschichold, Swansea University, UK
- Francis Tyers, The Arctic University of Norway, Norway
- Sowmya Vajjala, Iowa State University, US
- Paul Vogt, Tilburg University, Netherlands
- Elena Volodina, University of Gothenburg, Sweden
- Torsten Zesch, University of Duisburg-Essen, Germany
- Robert Östling, Stockholm University, Sweden

Workshop organizers,
Elena Volodina, Ildikó Pilán, Lars Borin (University of Gothenburg)
Gintare Grigonyte, Kristina Nilsson Björkenstam (Stockholm University)

Workshop website: <http://spraakbanken.gu.se/eng/research/icall/4thnlp4call>

Acknowledgements:
Financial support for the organization of the workshop has come from the University of Gothenburg, Språkbanken <https://spraakbanken.gu.se/>, and Swedish Research Council through its funding of the conference organization (Dnr. 2016-00447).

References

Josefsson, Gunlög. 2016. <http://www.svd.se/professor-snabbspar-till-svenska-fungerar-inte/om/debatt>. Svenska dagbladet. Retrieved 2016-02-22.

Heilman, M., Collins-Thompson, K., Callan, J. and Eskenazi, M. 2006. Classroom Success of an Intelligent Tutoring System for Lexical Practice and Reading Comprehension. ICSLP.

Detmar Meurers, Ramon Ziai, Luiz Amaral, Adriane Boyd, Aleksandar Dimitrov, Vanessa Metcalf, Niels Ott. 2010. Enhancing Authentic Web Pages for Language Learners. Proceedings of the 5th Workshop on Innovative Use of NLP for Building Educational Applications, NAACL-HLT 2010, Los Angeles.

Migrationsverket. 2016. http://www.migrationsverket.se/Om-Migrationsverket/Statistik/Aktuell-statistik.html

Mitkov, R. and Ha, L.A. 2003. Computer-Aided Generation of Multiple-Choice Tests. Proceedings of the HLT-NAACL 2003 Workshop on Building Educational Applications Using Natural Language Processing, 17-22.

Nerbonne, J. and Smit, P. (1996). GLOSSER-RuG: In Support of Reading. COLING-96. The 16th International Conference on Computational Linguistics. Proceedings, vol.2 830-835. Copenhagen: Centre for Sprogteknologi.

OECD. 2013. OECD Skills Outlook 2013. First Results from the Survey of Adult Skills. http://skills.oecd.org/skillsoutlook.html

PIAAC. 2013. http://www.oecd.org/site/piaac/

Robert Reynolds, Eduard Schaf and Detmar Meurers: A VIEW of Russian: Visual Input Enhancement and adaptive feedback. *Proceedings of the 3rd Workshop on NLP for Computer-Assisted Language Learning at the 5th Swedish Language Technology Conference*, Uppsala University, Sweden.

Skolverket. 2014. http://www.skolverket.se/skolutveckling/larande/nyanlandas-larande

SCB, Statistiska centralbyrån. 2013. Tema utbildning, rapport 2013:2, *Den internationella undersökningen av vuxnas färdigheter.* http://www.scb.se/statistik/_publikationer/UF0546_2013A01_BR_00_A40BR1302.pdf

Tufis, D. 1996. CALL: The Potential of Lingware and the Use of Empirical Linguistic Data. COLING - 96. The 16th international conference on computational linguistics. Proceedings, vol.2. 1010-1011. Copenhagen: Center for Språkteknologi.

Preben Wik & Anna Hjalmarsson. 2009. Embodied conversational agents in computer assisted language learning. *Speech communication* 51 (10), 1024-1037

From Distributions to Labels:
A Lexical Proficiency Analysis using Learner Corpora

David Alfter, Yuri Bizzoni, Anders Agebjörn, Elena Volodina, Ildikó Pilán
University of Gothenburg, Sweden
`{david.alfter,yuri.bizzoni,anders.agebjorn`
`elena.volodina,ildiko.pilan}@gu.se`

Abstract

This paper presents work on how we can link word lists derived from learner corpora to target proficiency levels for lexical complexity analysis. The word lists present frequency distributions over different proficiency levels. We present a mapping approach which takes these distributions and maps each word to a single proficiency level. We are also investigating how we can evaluate the mapping from distribution to proficiency level. We show that the distributional profile of words from the essays, informed with the essays' levels, consistently overlaps with our frequency-based method, in the sense that words holding the same level of proficiency as predicted by our mapping tend to cluster together in a semantic space. In the absence of a gold standard, this information can be useful to see how often a word is associated with the same level in two different models. Also, in this case we have a similarity measure that can show which words are more central to a given level and which words are more peripheral.

1 Introduction

In this work we look at how information from second language learner essay corpora can be used for the evaluation of unseen learner essays. Using a corpus of learner essays which have been graded by well-trained human assessors using the Common European Framework of Reference (CEFR) (Council of Europe, 2001), we extract a list of word distributions over CEFR levels. For the analysis of unseen essays, we want to map each word to a so-called *target* CEFR level using this word list.

The aim of this project is two-fold: first, we want to create a list of words linked to target proficiency levels. Second, we want to apply this list for lexical complexity analysis of unseen learner essays.

Most vocabulary lists used for second language learner evaluation, such as estimation of vocabulary size, are often derived from native speaker (L1) materials and thus might be ill suited to the needs of second language (L2) learners (François et al., 2016). It is hypothesized that second language learners need to focus on aspects of a language which are not present in native speaker materials (François et al., 2016).

However, such word lists are important for example in essay classification or lexical complexity analysis (Pilán et al., 2016; Volodina et al., 2016a). We thus base our approach on a learner corpus. From this corpus, we extract a list of words with their frequency distributions across proficiency levels. We then link each word to one single proficiency level. In contrast to traditional frequency based proficiency estimations, our approach includes information about learners. We look at "diversity" of a word, i.e. by how many different learners the word has been used at each level. We hypothesize that including diversity scores in the calculation of distribution-to-label mapping yields more reliable and plausible mappings.

The question that remains concerns evaluation. How can we measure the "accuracy" of our mapping in the absence of a gold standard? We address this problem by, on one hand, taking into account expert knowledge from teachers in order to refine the algorithms and, on the other hand, using a second separate approach to see to what extent both methods overlap.

The method we have chosen for evaluation is a semantic space approach. One of the advantages of the semantic space approach is that it gives us graded results; we can see to what *extent* words are similar to each other, possibly identifying core vocabulary and peripheral vocabulary at the different proficiency stages.

2   Related work

In the area of Swedish as a second language, several vocabulary lists have been created, such as SVALex (François et al., 2016), SweLL list (Llozhi, 2016), Kelly list (Kilgarriff et al., 2014), the Base Vocabulary Pool (Forsbom, 2006), SveVoc (Mühlenbock and Kokkinakis, 2012) and Swedish Academic Wordlist (Jansson et al., 2012). Of those lists, only SVALex, SweLL list and Kelly list attempted to link vocabulary items to the different proficiency levels according to the Common European Framework of Reference (CEFR) (Council of Europe, 2001), indicating at which level words should be introduced (François et al., 2016).

However, the Kelly list has been compiled from web texts intended for L1 speakers and the vocabulary used for first language (L1) speakers may differ from what beginner second language (L2) speakers need to concentrate on (François et al., 2016). Also, the division into the CEFR levels is based on frequency and the list lacks everyday words useful for learners of Swedish as a second language (François et al., 2016).

SVALex and SweLL list on the other hand have been derived from L2 Swedish material. SVALex has been compiled from the COCTAILL textbook corpus (Volodina et al., 2014) and focuses on receptive vocabulary, while SweLL list has been derived from the SweLL corpus (Volodina et al., 2016b), a corpus of L2 Swedish learner essays, and focuses on productive vocabulary. Neither of these lists link vocabulary items to CEFR levels, but present frequency distributions of lexical items over CEFR levels (Volodina et al., 2014; Volodina et al., 2016b).

In this work we try to use such word lists with frequency distributions over CEFR levels to assign a single CEFR label to each word. This information can be used to analyze texts and visualize the information from a lexical complexity perspective.

3   The learner corpus: SweLL

Our experiments are based on SweLL (Volodina et al., 2016b), a corpus of essays written by Swedish as a second language (L2) learners. The data covers five of the six CEFR levels, namely A1-C1. Table 2 shows the distribution of essays, sentences and tokens per level. Each essay has been manually labeled for CEFR levels by at least two L2 Swedish teachers. The inter-annotator agreement in terms of Krippendorff's alpha (Krippendorff, 1980) for assigning one of the five CEFR levels was 0.80 which reaches the threshold value specified in (Artstein and Poesio, 2008) for assuring a good annotation quality. Furthermore, the texts have been automatically annotated across different linguistic dimensions including lemmatization, part-of-speech (POS) tagging and dependency parsing using the Sparv (previously knows as 'Korp') pipeline (Borin et al., 2012). The essays encompass a variety of topics and genres and they are accompanied by meta-information on learners' mother tongue(s), age, gender, education level, the exam setting.

Level	Nr essays	Nr tokens
A1	16	2084
A2	83	18349
B1	76	30131
B2	74	32691
C1	90	60832
Total	**339**	**144 087**

Table 1: Number of items per CEFR level

4   Extracting the data

We extract a list of words and their frequency distributions over CEFR levels from the SweLL corpus. In contrast to the earlier SweLL list (Llozhi, 2016), we calculate relative frequencies for each level and extract further information such as learner counts and topics over levels.

Table 2 exemplifies the resulting data. In the first column, we have the lemma of a word, in the second column the corresponding part of speech, fol-

lemma	pos	A1	A2	B1	...	LI A1	LI A2	LI B1	...	T A1	T A2
göra	VB	0.12	0.23	0.61	...	x2, b1, a3, c7	x1, y1	z9	...	everyday life	...
...											
heta	VB	0.10	0.22	0.46	...	x1, b3, y6, z3	k2, l1, m1	n2, p1	...	personal info	...
...											

Table 2: Extracted data: Example

lowed by the distribution over the CEFR levels A1-C1. Then, we also have columns which indicate the learner IDs (indicated by LI A1, LI A2, etc.). These columns indicate which learner used the word at which level. This information is used when normalizing the data. Finally, we have columns which indicate the distribution of topics (T A1, T A2, etc.) for a given word over different levels. We plan on implementing topic modeling using this information at a later stage.

5 From distributions to labels

In order to link lexical items to CEFR levels, we have to define how we map from a frequency distribution over CEFR levels to a single level. The following sections describe the algorithm, the problem of why we can't directly map frequency distributions to labels, and word diversity normalization, which solves this problem.

5.1 Algorithm

In contrast to receptive vocabulary lists, the concept of 'target level', i.e. at which level a word should be understandable, is not applicable to word lists derived from productive vocabulary.

Instead we look at the *significant onset of use*, i.e. at which level a word is used significantly more often than at the preceding level.

In order to calculate the significant onset of use, for each word we calculate the score D_i at level i as the difference in frequencies between the current level i and the previous level $i-1$ as shown in equation 1. If $i = $ A1, $f_{i-1} = 0$.

$$D_i = |f_i - f_{i-1}| \qquad (1)$$

If D_i is higher than a certain threshold value, we take the level i as label for the word. Based on initial

empirical investigations with L2 teachers that rate the overlap between teacher- and system-assigned levels, we have found that a threshold value of 0.4 works well; lower threshold values exclude relevant words from a certain level while higher threshold values include words which are deemed to be of a different level.

5.2 The problem

If we look at the data, we can see that mapping distributions to labels is not straightforward, e.g. figures 1 and 2 show the distributions of the words *heta* (verb) 'to be called' and *göra* (verb) 'to do'. Using the *significant onset of use* algorithm, we would predict B1 as label for these words.

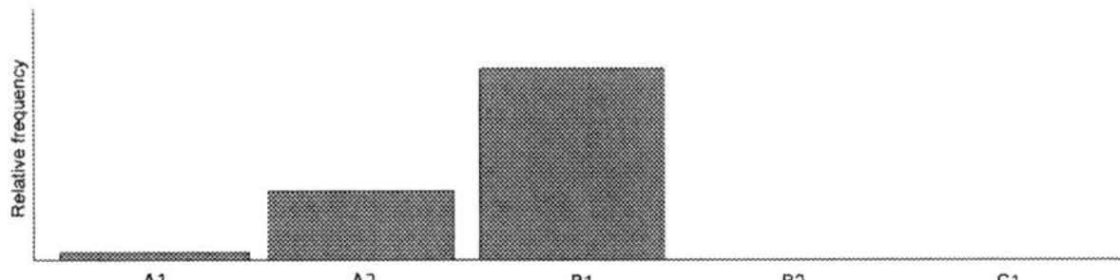

Figure 1: Frequency distribution of the word *heta* 'to be called'

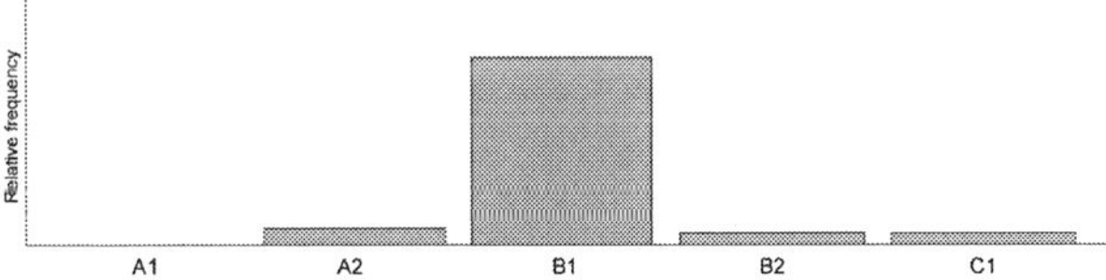

Figure 2: Frequency distribution of the word *göra* 'to do'

However, those words will most probably be used earlier by learners, since CEFR, inter alia, defines CEFR proficiency levels through topics. For example, the CEFR document states that one should be able to "introduce him/herself and others and [...] ask and answer questions about personal details such as where they live, people he/she knows and things he/she has" (Council of Europe, 2001, page 24).

The verbs *göra* and *heta* are encountered very often at the beginner level as beginners learn to introduce themselves (e.g. *Jag heter Peter.* 'My name is Peter.') and talk about things they do.

Thus, common sense dictates that we cannot simply use frequency distributions as indicators of when learners should be assumed to be able to start using certain words productively.

5.3 Word diversity

In contrast to directly mapping frequency distributions to labels, we have found that normalizing the frequencies using *word diversity* improved results significantly. We calculate word diversity for each word by looking at how often the word was used at each level and how many *different* learners used the word at each level. Word diversity of a word w at level L is calculated by dividing the number of occurrences of the word at level L by the number of distinct learners d that used the word at that level as shown in equation 2. The intuition is that if a word is used often at a certain level, but only by one learner, it is less representative of this level than if it is used by many different learners.

$$diversity(w, L) = \frac{count(w, L)}{count(d, w, L)} \quad (2)$$

After normalizing the original frequency distribution to fit into the interval 0-1, we average the word diversity distribution and the normalized frequency distribution to arrive at a new distribution. Figure 3 shows the new distribution for *heta*.

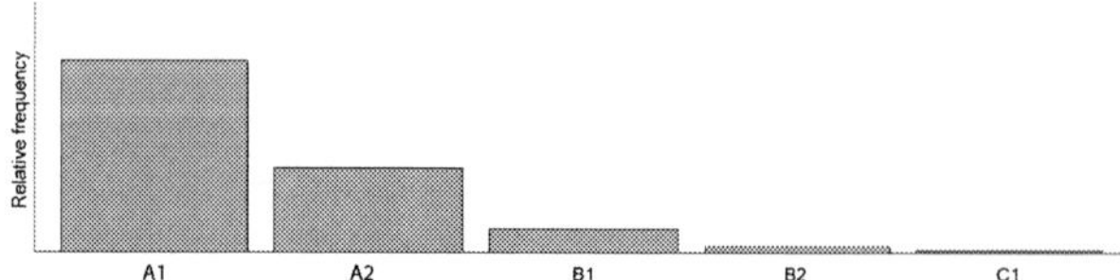

Figure 3: New distribution of the word *heta* 'to be called'

We can see that including word diversity shifts the original frequency distribution towards the left, with a peak at A1. Incidentally, the automatically predicted level for this word is also A1; however, it should be noted that the calculation of the significant onset of use differs from simply taking the peak. For example, figure 4 shows the recalculated distribution for the relatively common verb *göra* 'to do'. We can see maxima at A2 and B2, but the algorithm predicts the more plausible A1.

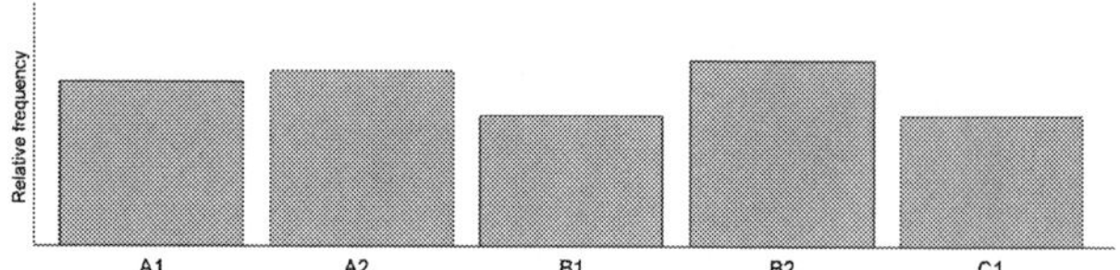

Figure 4: New distribution of the word *göra* 'to do'

6 Distributional semantics

We used the gensim implementation of Word2Vec (Mikolov and Dean, 2013) to create a vector space model of our corpus of essays. Since we don't have a gold standard to validate our results, we wanted to see to what extent we might reproduce the same essay level labeling through a different method. We have 339 essays, each one labeled with a CEFR grade as assigned by a teacher. Given this data, we built two different kinds of semantic spaces: a simple context-based space taking into account a number of words at the left and right of the given lemma; and an "indexed" approach which, for each word in an essay, takes into account both its context and the proficiency level of the whole essay. In other terms, the proficiency level of an essay is treated as contextual information to build a word's distributional vector, in the same way as other words. We also tried a stricter approach where we constrained the system to take into consideration only the proficiency level to build the distributional vector of a lemma, under the assumption that words sharing the same proficiency-related distributional profile would tendentially cluster together in a semantic space, without need for further information.

It is important to understand what kind of spaces these approaches create. If we don't take proficiency levels directly into account, we generate a traditional semantic space where words that have similar contexts cluster together. The problem in creating consistent proficiency-related vocabularies with this approach is clear: if a C1 word happens to be a synonym of an A1 word (and thus used in similar contexts) it will be more similar to such A1 word than to other C1 words.

If we take into account both context and proficiency levels, proficiency level labels become themselves "points" in the multidimensional semantic space: thus, words that occur in the same level will tend to be near, but also a word will be nearer to the proficiency label it shares most context with. The advantage of this method is that we can directly compute the similarity between a lemma and a proficiency level; the disadvantage is that contextual information could actually work as noise. For example, if a complex word as *angelägenheter* 'concerns' (noun) co-occurs with a simple word as *tisdag* 'Tuesday', and *tisdag* mainly happens at level A1, then *angelägenheter* and the point 'A1' will become closer.

If, finally, we only take into account the proficiency level, words that occur in the same level will be similar in the semantic space. In this case we cannot meaningfully compute a word-level similarity but the risks of contextual noise are reduced. It can be interesting to note that since we are using a continuous semantic space we can try to predict the proficiency level (in a direct or indirect way) of full documents by averaging the individual vectors of their words.

We can use one of these models to compute the direct cosine similarity between a word and a level and that we could use to check whether the most similar words to a given level, e.g. B1, are the same we labeled as B1 in our frequency-based approach. On the other hand we can use the other model to see whether words cluster together consistently with our frequency based lists.

7 Evaluation

The first reason we used a semantic space to model L2 essays vocabulary is to see whether, using a different approach, we might obtain results consistent with the frequency-based learner-augmented lists we described in the first part of the paper. As we explained, we don't expect simple distributional models to work very well on this task, but we tried to monitor the performance of a so-called "indexed method" to try to make words characteristic of specific proficiency level closer between them and to the level label itself in the semantic space. If a semantic space model trained as described above reproduces the predictions of our frequency-based lists (for example clustering together words that are in the

same proficiency level in the lists) we could be a little more confident that our labeling is sensible. To test this we randomly selected 100 words from our frequency lists, equally distributed among the 5 proficiency classes A1-C1. On these 100 words we ran two tests: one based on the word-label cosine similarity, and one based on the word-word cosine similarity. The first test selects, in the semantic space, the nearest proficiency label to a given word. For example given the word *eftersom* 'because', we select the label holding the nearest cosine similarity with it, for example "A2"; if *eftersom* is mapped to the level A2 according to our mapping algorithm, we have an agreement among our models. We can then count how many "nearest labels" coincided with the frequency-based prediction and determine to what extent the two approaches are consistent in modeling the data.

The second test consists in simply retrieving, for every word, its *n*-nearest neighbours in the semantic space. We can then determine whether these neighbours belong to the same proficiency level of the given word in the frequency list. For example, we can retrieve the nearest neighbours of the word *tisdag* 'Tuesday' and find them to be *lördag* 'Saturday' and *trött* 'tired'. If these two words are of the same proficiency level as *tisdag* in our lists, we can suppose a certain consistency between the two approaches.

Table 3 shows the results for the different tests and different models. We tested two indexed models, with window size 1 and 60 respectively, and a non-indexed model with window size 10. The numbers indicate how many items were assigned the same proficiency levels in both the semantic space model and the frequency-based mapping, with the upper limit being 100. We are indicating counts, but as the upper limit is 100, the numbers can also be understood as percentages. For the word-word similarity test, we look at the first, second and third most similar words according to the cosine similarity and check whether their proficiency label is the same as the one assigned by the frequency-based mapping. The figures in parentheses indicate the number of *close mismatches* (off-by-one errors).

Apparently, an "indexed" semantic space with a large window shows the highest agreement with our model. Considering that we are predicting labels

	word-label test	word-word similarity test (n-nearest neighbours)		
		1st nearest	2nd nearest	3rd nearest
Indexed model (w=1)	33 (29)	35 (36)	27 (46)	34 (37)
Indexed model (w=60)	**51** (13)	**67** (31)	**44** (37)	**46** (37)
Non-indexed model (w=10)	18 (31)	38 (38)	24 (49)	28 (34)

Table 3: Results

over five proficiency levels, accuracies of 51% and 67% are encouraging numbers. What is maybe even more interesting is the number of *close mismatches*. These cases are interesting because they could show that the models are setting different boundaries, but tendentially agree on the general progression of the vocabulary. If the number of close mismatches is high, it means that we have many cases where A1 words (in our frequency list) are "labeled" as, or cluster with, A2 words in the semantic space: it is easy to see that similar cases are qualitatively very different from cases where an A1 word clusters with C1 vocabulary. The large presence of similar cases in our results brings us the next reason that induced us to use semantic spaces: they can give nuanced results. If we use a distributional space to label a lemma, we'll have not only the most probable level of such lemma, but also its distance to the next and previous level. For example, both our frequency list and our best performing semantic space label *resa* 'to travel' as an A2 word. From the semantic space, we can also see that it is much closer to B1 than to A1 – we can suppose that it is a rather "advanced" word that tends to lie between A2 and B1. In the same way, *fredag* 'Friday', labeled as A2 by the frequency lists, clusters in our space both with A2 and (less closely) A1 lemmas, showing that it is likely to be a term on the "easy" spectrum of the A2 vocabulary.

8 Lexical complexity analysis

In order to analyze an unseen learner essay, we annotate the essay using the Sparv pipeline (Borin et al., 2012). This step results in a lemmatized and part-of-speech tagged text. Each lemma is then looked up in the previously calculated word list and marked as being of the level indicated in the word list.

We can then simply visualize this information using a graphical user interface[1] as shown in figure 5. After entering a text in the text box, it is possible to highlight words of certain CEFR levels. This kind of visualization can give a good impression of the distribution of word levels in a text.

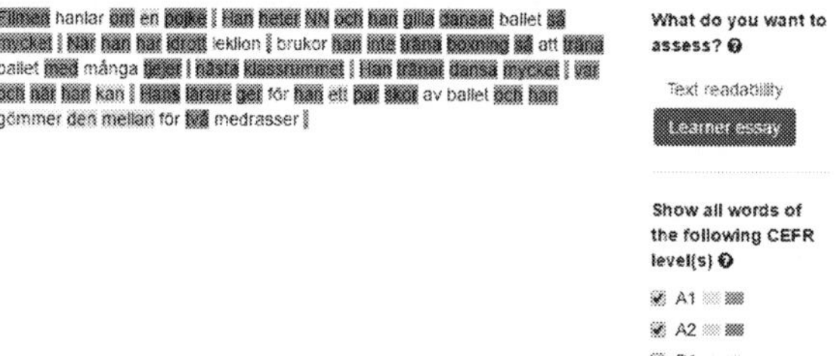

Figure 5: Text evaluation: Visualization

We can also use the word list to predict the overall proficiency level of the essay. Rather than being used on its own, it is incorporated into larger systems. Recent research has shown that substituting traditional frequency based lists by distributionally mapped word lists in machine learning based automatic essay grading systems results in significantly better predictions (Pilán et al., 2016).

9 Conclusion

In this paper we have shown how lists of frequency distributions of lexical items over CEFR levels can be used for lexical complexity analysis by linking each word to a single CEFR label. We have found that augmenting frequency based lists with learner counts yields more plausible mappings than taking into account only the frequency information. Using a semantic space approach we have shown that our results are consistent across different models. Finally, we have shown how this information can be visualized and used for essay grade prediction.

---

[1] https://spraakbanken.gu.se/larkalabb/texteval

References

R. Artstein and M. Poesio. 2008. Inter-coder agreement for computational linguistics. *Computational Linguistics*, 34(4):555–596.

Lars Borin, Markus Forsberg, and Johan Roxendal. 2012. Korp - the corpus infrastructure of Språkbanken. In *LREC*, pages 474–478.

Council of Europe. 2001. *Common European Framework of Reference for Languages: Learning, Teaching, Assessment*. Press Syndicate of the University of Cambridge.

Eva Forsbom. 2006. A swedish base vocabulary pool. In *Swedish Language Technology conference, Gothenburg*.

Thomas François, Elena Volodina, Ildikó Pilán, and Anaïs Tack. 2016. SVALex: a CEFR-graded Lexical Resource for Swedish Foreign and Second Language Learners. In *LREC 2016*.

Håkan Jansson, Sofie Johansson Kokkinakis, Judy Ribeck, and Emma Sköldberg. 2012. A Swedish Academic Word List: Methods and Data. In *Proceedings of the 15th EURALEX International Congress*, pages 7–11.

Adam Kilgarriff, Frieda Charalabopoulou, Maria Gavrilidou, Janne Bondi Johannessen, Saussan Khalil, Sofie Johansson Kokkinakis, Robert Lew, Serge Sharoff, Ravikiran Vadlapudi, and Elena Volodina. 2014. Corpus-based vocabulary lists for language learners for nine languages. *Language resources and evaluation*, 48(1):121–163.

K. Krippendorff. 1980. *Content Analysis: An Introduction to Its Methodology. Chapter 12*. Sage, Beverly Hills, CA.

Lorena Llozhi. 2016. SweLL list. A list of productive vocabulary generated from second language learners' essays. Master's Thesis. University of Gothenburg.

Tomas Mikolov and Jeff Dean. 2013. Distributed representations of words and phrases and their compositionality. *Advances in neural information processing systems*.

Katarina Heimann Mühlenbock and Sofie Johansson Kokkinakis. 2012. SweVoc-a Swedish vocabulary resource for CALL. In *Proceedings of the SLTC 2012 workshop on NLP for CALL; Lund; 25th October; 2012*, number 080, pages 28–34. Linköping University Electronic Press.

Ildikó Pilán, David Alfter, and Elena Volodina. 2016. Coursebook texts as a helping hand for classifying linguistic complexity in language learners' writings. In *Proceedings of the workshop on Computational Linguistics for Linguistic Complexity (CL4LC)*. COLING 2016. Osaka, Japan.

Elena Volodina, Ildikó Pilán, Stian Rødven Eide, and Hannes Heidarsson. 2014. You get what you annotate: a pedagogically annotated corpus of coursebooks for Swedish as a Second Language. In *Proceedings of the third workshop on NLP for computer-assisted language learning at SLTC 2014, Uppsala University*, number 107. Linköping University Electronic Press.

Elena Volodina, Ildikó Pilán, and David Alfter. 2016a. Classification of Swedish learner essays by CEFR levels. In *Proceedings of EuroCALL 2016*.

Elena Volodina, Ildikó Pilán, Ingegerd Enström, Lorena Llozhi, Peter Lundkvist, Gunlög Sundberg, and Monica Sandell. 2016b. SweLL on the rise: Swedish Learner Language corpus for European Reference Level studies. In *LREC 2016*.

Towards error annotation in a learner corpus of Portuguese

Iria del Río[1], Sandra Antunes[1], Amália Mendes[1] and Maarten Janssen[2]

[1] University of Lisbon – CLUL
[2] University of Coimbra – CELGA-ILTEC
iagayo@gmail.com, sandra.antunes@clul.ul.pt,
amalia.mendes@clul.ul.pt, maartenpt@gmail.com

Abstract

In this article, we present COPLE2, a new corpus of Portuguese that encompasses written and spoken data produced by foreign learners of Portuguese as a foreign or second language (FL/L2). Following the trend towards learner corpus research applied to less commonly taught languages, it is our aim to enhance the learning data of Portuguese L2. These data may be useful not only for educational purposes (design of learning materials, curricula, etc.) but also for the development of NLP tools to support students in their learning process. The corpus is available online using TEITOK environment, a web-based framework for corpus treatment that provides several built-in NLP tools and a rich set of functionalities (multiple orthographic transcription layers, lemmatization and POS, normalization of the tokens, error annotation) to automatically process and annotate texts in xml format. A CQP-based search interface allows searching the corpus for different fields, such as words, lemmas, POS tags or error tags. We will describe the work in progress regarding the constitution and linguistic annotation of this corpus, particularly focusing on error annotation.

1   Introduction

The COPLE2 corpus[1] is a written and spoken learner corpus of Portuguese as a foreign or second language (FL/L2) that aims at providing empirical data for the teaching and learning of this language. Several learner corpora have been compiled for English, such as the International Corpus of Learner English (Granger et al., 2009), the Longman Learner's Corpus, or the Cambridge Learner Corpus (Nicholls, 2003). The importance of such empirical data has been increasingly recognized for studies in Second Language Acquisition and language teaching/learning. Recently, we have seen a substantial growth in this area regarding other languages besides English. Concerning Romance languages, there are already some corpora and resources for French (Delais-Roussarie & Yoo, 2010), Spanish (Lozano, 2009) and Italian (Boyd et al., 2014). In the case of the Portuguese language, there are also some initiatives in the compilation of learner corpora. The corpus *Recolha de dados de Aprendizagem do Português Língua Estrangeira*[2], that follows the precursor work developed in Leiria (2001), was compiled at the School of Arts and Humanities of the University of Lisbon, and includes 470 texts and 70,500 tokens. The *Corpus de Produções Escritas de Aprendentes de PL2*[3], compiled at the University of Coimbra, is constituted by 516 texts and 119,381 tokens. Finally, the *Corpus de Aquisição de L2*[4], compiled at the New University of Lisbon, contains 281,301 words, and it includes texts produced by adults and children, as well as a spoken subset. Following these previous projects, we believe that COPLE2 corpus will contribute to broaden this emerging

---

[1] http://www.clul.ul.pt/en/research-teams/547

[2] http://www.clul.ul.pt/pt/recursos/314-corpora-of-ple
[3] http://www.uc.pt/fluc/rcpl2/
[4] http://cal2.clunl.edu.pt/

domain by enhancing the learning data of Portuguese. COPLE2 makes use of a large set of learner texts (from different mother tongues (L1s) and proficiency levels) and, in contrast to the corpora mentioned above, it is linguistically interpreted with information on lemma and POS. Furthermore, it provides rich TEI annotation of the actual writing, the normalization of the orthography and error corrections, as well as a powerful multilayer query options.

We will first introduce the corpus and the interface tool in sections 2 and 3, respectively: section 2 presents the COPLE2 corpus, its design and the transcription process of written and spoken data, while section 3 gives an overview of the visualization and search options provided by the interface tool. In section 4, we introduce the error annotation system, the tagset and the discussion about the distribution of errors.

2 The COPLE2 corpus

COPLE2 corpus is constituted by written and spoken Portuguese learning data produced by students that attended Portuguese FL/L2 courses (annual or summer) at the School of Arts and Humanities of the University of Lisbon[5], and by applicants to accreditation exams, between 2010 and 2014.

2.1 Corpus Design and Metadata

The written subpart of COPLE2 currently contains 966 free essays, in a total of 156,691 tokens, produced by 424 students that represent 14 different L1s. We only selected L1s that had a minimum of 6 informants in our initial data set (cf. Table 1).

L1	Inf.	Texts	L1	Inf.	Texts
Chinese	129	323	Italian	20	34
English	65	142	Dutch	11	15
Spanish	52	139	Terum	9	22
German	39	76	Polish	8	22
Russian	25	70	Arabic	8	13
Japanese	23	50	Korean	6	9
French	23	43	Romanian	6	8

Table 1: Informants and texts of the written subcorpus.

Given the heterogeneous nature of the informants, we registered detailed metadata regarding both the learner and the task profiles. Thus, concerning the learner's profile, we established a set of 8 required fields: name, age (18-40 years old), gender, mother tongue, nationality, proficiency based on the Common European Framework of Reference for Languages[6] (A1 (7%), A2 (40%), B1 (31%), B2 (19%), C1 (3%)), knowledge of other foreign languages and period of time studying Portuguese.

The text profile includes fields on: genre (argumentative (35,5%), narrative (17,5%), personal letter (12,5%), formal letter (10,5%), informative (9,6%), dialogue (6,4%), message/e-mail (6,3%), retell a story (1,5%) and literary critic (0,2%)), topic, task description (diagnostic test, mid-term or final test, homework, accreditation exam), timebound or not, with access to reference books or not, number of tokens and date.

Regarding the spoken subpart, the compilation of this subcorpus is still in progress. At the moment, 12 recordings are transcribed. The recordings consist on conversations between 2 or 3 learners of different proficiency levels moderated by the examiner, on topics such as: (i) presentation of the students; (ii) simulation of communicative situations; (iii) discussion of particular subjects, presenting arguments and opinions.

The metadata of the spoken task also encode information on the recording situation, such as: total time of the recording, total time of the segment that is transcribed and the location of the transcribed segment, acoustic quality, hidden or visible recording, involvement of the evaluator (dialogue, monologue or monologue with few interactions), spontaneous or planned, elicitation or non elicitation, social context (family, private, public, controlled environment) and channel (face to face, experimental, media, phone conversations, etc.).

Table 2 shows the current contents of the corpus per level and per modality.

[5] The corpus compilation is funded by Fundação para a Ciência e Tecnologia (UID/LIN/00214/2013), Fundação Calouste Gulbenkian (Proc. nr. 134655) and ADFLUL.

[6] Council of Europe (2001).

Level	Written		Spoken		Total	
	Texts	Tokens	Texts	Tokens	Texts	Tokens
A1	72	6,438	10	18,803	82	25,241
A2	382	49,761	0	0	382	49,761
B1	305	53,042	0	0	305	53,042
B2	181	39,665	1	3,010	182	42,675
C1	26	7,785	1	3,970	27	11,755
Total	**966**	**156,691**	**12**	**25,783**	**978**	**182,474**

Table 2: COPLE2 design.

2.2 Data Transcription

The hand-written essays were first scanned and saved in pdf format, and then manually transcribed. The transcriptions are encoded in TEI compliant XML (Burnard & Bauman, 2013). Each file is composed by a header (with the metadata mentioned above) and the transcription, as illustrated in Figure 1, below.

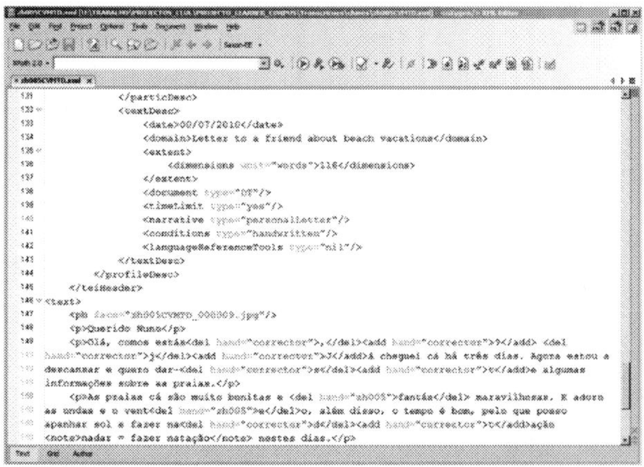

Figure 1: Part of a written transcription following XML.

The written transcriptions are very close to the original document in the sense that all the changes made by the student during the writing process (such as deletions, additions, transposition of segments, etc.) were also encoded. This information is extremely useful to assess, for instance, the difficult areas for the learning process according to the student's L1, the discourse restructuring or errors triggered by homophone words. In addition, all the corrections and comments made by the teacher were also transcribed. Teacher's feedback can be useful for future pedagogical studies and, as we will explain below, it constitutes a valuable support for error identification in the error annotation process. All personal information (such as names, addresses, phone numbers) were anonymized (Hinrichs, 2006).

Regarding the spoken corpus, the recordings were transcribed following CHILDES (MacWhinney, 2000) and C-ORAL-ROM (Cresti and Moneglia, 2005) guidelines, which favours a transcription based on prosody. Thus, instead of punctuation marks, we used symbols that represent intonation. Also, all the speech disfluencies (such as fragmented words, false starts, filled pauses and other non-lexical utterances) were transcribed. All the transcriptions were text-to-sound aligned using the EXMARaLDA editor (Schmidt, 2012).

3 TEITOK Interface Tool

After completion of the transcriptions, all the files were imported into the Tokenized TEI Environment – TEITOK[7] for visualization, linguistic annotation and search functions (Janssen, 2012; 2016). This system makes it easy to display XML files, edit metadata and individual tokens, and perform complex searches through the corpus.

The corpus was firstly automatically tokenized, which means that all lexical words and contracted words (such as prepositions contracted with articles, demonstratives, etc.) were identified (e.g. $naquele = em_{preposition}$ 'in' + $aquele_{demonstrative}$ 'that one'). The automatic POS annotation and lemmatization were performed, using the Neotag tagger (Janssen, 2012), which was trained over a gold standard subset of the Reference Corpus of Contemporary Portuguese (Mendes et al., 2014). For error tagging purposes, as we will see in the next section, a normalized version (orthographic, lexical or syntactic) may be provided also for each token. Because learner errors affect automatic POS tagging and lemmatization, default POS and lemma are normalized, that is, corrected when needed and stored at the first level of error annotation (orthographic). We will come back to this intersection of POS and error annotation in section 4.

Afterwards, for the written subcorpus, TEITOK interprets the XML encoding (CSS rules define how to display the XML elements) to enable the visualization of different versions of the text: (i) the XML version; (ii) the transcription version

---

[7] http://alfclul.clul.ul.pt/teitok/site/index.php?action=about

(visualization close to the full information of the XML document); (iii) the student form, which corresponds to the final version intended by the student; (iv) the corrected form, which displays the teacher corrections; (v) the error-annotated form; (vi) the image of the handwritten essay, on request. Each version has a specific separator, and all the changes made to the original student text are displayed in different colours. Figure 2 shows the teacher's correction version, where the corrected words are in red.

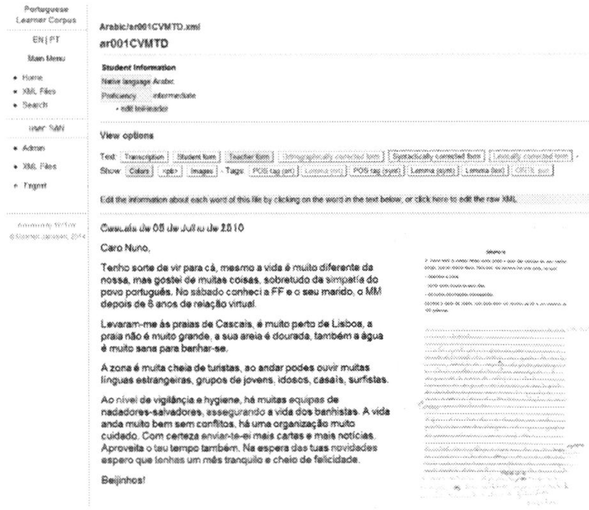

Figure 2: Visualization of the correction of a written essay.

All this information can be also displayed when moving the mouse over the words in the text. Figure 3 shows a misspelled word with the respective correction and all the linguistic information.

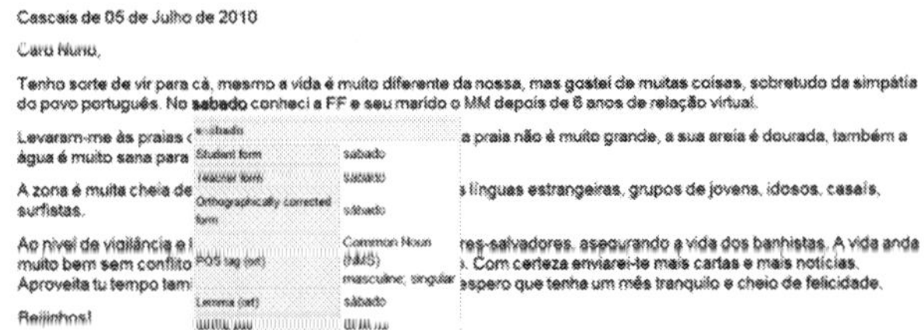

Figure 3: Highlighted word with linguistic information.

Regarding the spoken transcriptions, EXMARaL-DA files were converted into TEI format. The spoken transcriptions are visualized as speech turns with a link to the audio sequence (cf. Figure 4).

Figure 4: Visualization of a recording transcription.

TEITOK allows for multi-token annotation (POS, lemma, error-annotation) with the possibility of using regular expressions when specific replacements have to be made.

Finally, the TEITOK environment also provides corpus search facilities using CQP (Christ et al., 1999). In the creation of the CQP corpus, various types of encoded information can be exported: metadata, POS, lemma, original orthography, normalized orthography, error annotations and the teacher corrections. This way, searches can combine all these different types of information, making it possible to perform complex and powerful search queries (cf. Figure 5).

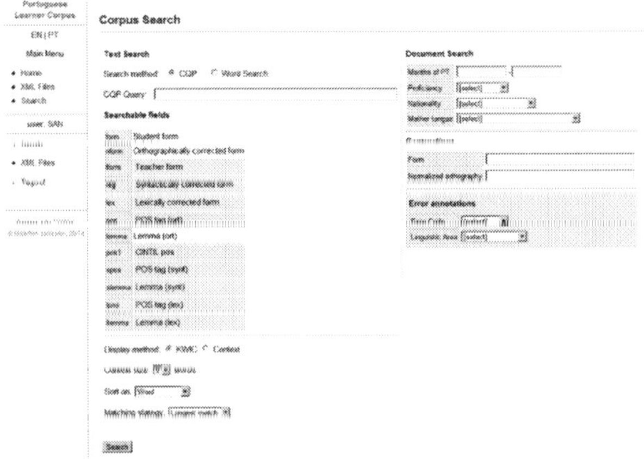

Figure 5: TEITOK query system.

The next step is to label the data following a typological scheme for error annotation (Tono, 2003; Nicholls, 2003; Dagneaux et al., 2005), as we describe in further detail below.

4 Error Annotation

Error tagging is an important step in learner corpora annotation since it helps to identify problematic areas in the learning process (Granger, 2004). Despite this fact, error tagging is not always present in learner corpora. There can be many possible reasons for that, but we can identify at least two important causes:

1. It is a high time-consuming task, that most of the times has to be performed manually.

2. There is no standard for error tagging and, in general, taxonomies are a result of particular projects with specific interests (Díaz-Negrillo & Fernández-Domíguez, 2006). As a consequence, an error taxonomy and an annotation paradigm have to be defined for each learner corpus and this is not a trivial task (Meurers, 2015), since it entails several complex sub-tasks like: define what an error is and what types of errors are considered; decide which is the scope of a given error (one word vs. multiple words); determine if corrections are provided or not; etc.

As we will show, in the case of COPLE2 we have tried to take advantage of the corpus architecture and the possibilities that the TEITOK environment offers to overtake the problems above.

There are examples of learner corpora with error annotation for many languages but, to the best of our knowledge, none of the learner corpora for Portuguese offers error annotation. Therefore, error tagging in COPLE2 constitutes the first attempt of this type of encoding for the Portuguese language.

4.1 Error annotation system in COPLE2

The error annotation paradigm in COPLE2 exploits the possibilities provided by the TEITOK environment. We have already described different levels of annotation that TEITOK allows for each token in the corpus (student form of the token *versus* teacher form of the token). For error tagging, we have defined three linguistic levels of annotation: orthographical, grammatical and lexical. In all the cases, the annotation consists on the addition of the correct word form with its lemma and POS. The three levels can be filled for a given token at the same time.

The first level is used if there is a spelling error in the student production. The orthographically corrected form (*nform*) is introduced, as well as the corresponding POS (*pos*) and lemma (*lemma*).

Figure 6 below shows an example of an orthographical error, where the student wrote *novedades* instead of *novidades* ('news').

Token value (w-174): novidades

XML	Raw XML value	nov<del hand="corrector">e</del>‹
form	Student form	novedades
fform	Teacher form	novidades
nform	Orthographically corrected form	novidades
reg	Syntactically corrected form	
lex	Lexically corrected form	
pos	POS tag (ort)	NFP
lemma	Lemma (ort)	novidade
spos	POS tag (synt)	
slemma	Lemma (synt)	
lpos	POS tag (lex)	
llemma	Lemma (lex)	
error	Error code(s)	

Figure 6: Annotation of an orthographic error.

As we have mentioned above, this first level contains the default POS and lemma for each token, which are corrected (normalized) when needed.

The second level operates if there is a grammatical error, that is: the word used by the student generates an ungrammatical utterance. Figure 7 shows an example: the student wrote *um cidade* ('a$_{\text{MASC}}$ city') instead of *uma cidade* ('a$_{\text{FEM}}$ city'), therefore, there is an agreement error which is annotated in the token corresponding to *um*. The syntactically corrected form is introduced (*reg*) as well as the corresponding POS (*spos*).

Token value (w-17): uma

XML	Raw XML value	um<add hand="corrector">a</add>
form	Student form	um
fform	Teacher form	uma
nform	Orthographically corrected form	
reg	Syntactically corrected form	uma
lex	Lexically corrected form	
pos	POS tag (ort)	BUMS
lemma	Lemma (ort)	um
spos	POS tag (synt)	BUFS
slemma	Lemma (synt)	
lpos	POS tag (lex)	
llemma	Lemma (lex)	
error	Error code(s)	

Figure 7: Annotation of a grammatical error.

Note that in this case the field *slemma* is not annotated. The reason is that there is inheritance between levels, from the bottom (orthographic data) to the top (lexical data), that is: *form > nform > reg*

> *lex*; *pos* > *spos* > *lpos*; *lemma* > *slemma* > *llemma*, and only what is new has to be annotated. Therefore, if *nform* is empty, the system reads that its value is the same as *form* (there is no inheritance from the teacher's correction, *fform*). If *reg* is filled in and *lex* is empty, the value for the *lex* is the same as for *reg*; and the same for the POS and the lemma. In the example in Figure 7, the value for *slemma* is the same as the value in *lemma*, and therefore *slemma* is empty. This is another advantage of the annotation system provided by TEITOK: the annotator only needs to annotate what is different, and not all the fields at each level.

Finally, the third level is used if there is a lexical/semantic error in the student form, i.e., the word can be grammatically correct, but it is not the natural word that a native speaker would use. Figure 8 shows an example where the student used the word *tropas* ('troops') in a context where *equipas* ('teams') was more adequate.

Token value (w-130): tropas equipas

XML	Raw XML value	`<del hand="corrector">tropas</del>`
form	Student form	tropas
fform	Teacher form	equipas
nform	Orthographically corrected form	
reg	Syntactically corrected form	
lex	Lexically corrected form	equipas
pos	POS tag (ort)	NFP
lemma	Lemma (ort)	tropa
spos	POS tag (synt)	
slemma	Lemma (synt)	
lpos	POS tag (lex)	
llemma	Lemma (lex)	oquipa
error	Error code(s)	

Figure 8: Annotation of a lexical error.

Again, in Figure 8, only *llemma* is annotated, because its value is different from the one in *lemma*; *lpos* has the same value as *pos* and, therefore, it remains empty.

The different levels provide also different visualizations of the text, where the introduced corrections replace the student forms. This way, it is possible to visualize the same text corrected at different levels, from the closer version to the original (only orthographic corrections) to the most modified one (orthographical, grammatical and lexical corrections).

The system described is a multi-tier annotation system, similar to the one presented in Rosen et al. (2013). Like in the Corpus of Czech as a Second Language, we define different levels of annotation that work bottom-up, where different representations of the learner form take place. As we can see, there is a hierarchy in the level of interpretation assumed by the annotator at each tier, from errors with clear boundaries (orthographical and grammatical) to errors more open to interpretation (lexical ones), where it is sometimes hard to determine the "naturalness" of a given utterance. In our system, we assume a target hypothesis (Meurers, 2015) where the reference linguistic system is the target native language. At each tier, different transformations are applied to produce the equivalent native language form:

- Orthographical level: the operations at this level are restricted to the word form and to punctuation marks. Punctuation, spelling and word boundaries problems are fixed, trying to generate the closest native form to the learner form. We include at this level problems in inflectional or derivational suffixes, like in the learner form *estabilitamos*, instead of *estabelecemos* ((we) 'establish'). The final interpreted form is a valid word in the native language.

- Grammatical level: the operations at this level are related to grammatical problems, that is, errors that go beyond the word and affect syntactic structures. Therefore, the annotator has to take into account the context surrounding the error. Examples are agreement problems (subject-verb, determiner-noun, noun-modifier, etc.), problems in the verb form (incorrect verbal tense, mode, etc.), subcategorization problems or problems in the POS selection. The final interpreted form allows for a grammatically correct structure in the learner production.

- Lexical level: the operations allowed at this level affect mainly meaning. The word used by the learner is orthographically and grammatically correct, but it is not the most natural choice for a native speaker (see above the example of *tropas* in Figure 8).

Because it works at the level of the token, this annotation system does not work for errors that affect more than one word, like word order errors or errors in multi-word expressions. For those cases, we will use stand-off annotation, which is already implemented in TEITOK (Janssen, 2016).

Currently, we are testing this annotation system, which seems intuitive and fast for the annotators. As part of the testing, we plan to perform inter-annotator agreement evaluation, to check the degree of confidence of the system. Considering the results showed by previous works like Rosen et al. (2013), we expect to find a relation between the annotator agreement and the level of interpretation allowed by the annotation tier (less interpretation at the orthographic and grammatical level, more interpretation at the lexical level). For the identification of errors, we plan to combine automatic and manual strategies, taking advantage of the information already encoded in the corpus, for example, teacher's corrections (always reviewed by a human annotator).

4.2 Distribution of errors: preliminary data

We do not have yet quantitative data about the total number of errors per type in the corpus but we have some indicative numbers from a pilot experiment we performed when we were designing a pilot taxonomy of errors. For this experiment we annotate 36 texts (7,073 tokens), trying to include all the languages in the corpus and, if possible, all the language levels. We found 591 errors (8.35% of total tokens), with the following distribution:

Type of error	Absolute Freq.	Percent Freq.
Orthographical	260	43.99
Grammatical	305	51.61
Lexical	26	4.4
Total	591	100

Table 3: Distribution of errors in a corpus sample.

As we expected, the most common errors are grammatical ones, followed by orthographic errors. This tendency was also showed for French in the FRIDA corpus in Granger 2003. On the other hand, lexical errors seem to be not very frequent, especially if the annotator is not very strict with the lexical choices of the learner.

4.3 Tagset of errors

As a further step, we plan to introduce error codes for each error annotated following the system described above. As we will see, the multi-tier error annotation will provide us automatically with the first level of information in the code, with a coarse-grained error annotation of the token.

We are working on the definition of the tagset that will be used, similar to the taxonomies described in Tono, (2003), Nicholls (2003) or Dagneaux et al. (2005). So far, we have defined a pilot tagset that will be applied to the corpus to test its performance. The current tagset has 37 tags and it is structured in two levels of information:
1 General linguistic area affected.
2 Error category (and subcategories in some cases).

For level 1 we consider the three linguistic areas that we have described above: Orthographic (includes spelling and punctuation errors), Grammatical (includes agreement errors; errors affecting verb tense, mode, etc.) and Lexical (includes lexical choice errors; errors affecting derivational suffixes; etc.). As we will show below, the use of the same general linguistic areas to classify the errors allows for transferring information between the multi-tier system and the code system. For level 2 we have common categories like agreement or wrong POS.

To design the tagset we performed the annotation experiment that we referred above, identifying the errors in those 36 texts and defining the necessary categories to annotate them. Besides the phenomena we observed in the annotated sample, we included also other phenomena that we expect to find in the corpus, considering other tagsets developed for similar projects. When defining the error categories, we decided to be as general as possible, trying to avoid restricting ourselves to specific theoretical frameworks or being too detailed. We think that it is always easier to manage general categories that can be sub-specified in later stages than to apply from the beginning very detailed linguistic categories. The tags we defined are position-based tags, where the first letter corresponds to level 1 and the subsequent letters to level 2. For example, for agreement errors affecting gender, we have the tag "GAG" which stands for "Grammar + Agreement + Gender". Since the error tag is added to the affected token/group of tokens in the xml, which include POS information, we do not include the POS information in the label.

We expect that the tagset will provide a fine-grained classification of errors, which in turn will allow for more specific queries concerning different linguistic phenomena (agreement, word order, use of incorrect POS, etc.). When possible, we will use all the information encoded for each token in COPLE2 to assign the error code automatically, comparing the original form from the student with the corrections (plus lemma and POS) introduced at the error annotation level. The first letter of the error code will be automatically assigned, taking into account the level where the error was annotated in the multi-tier system (orthographic, grammatical or lexical). The subsequent letters corresponding to the error type will be assigned automatically when possible. For example: if there is an annotated form at *nform* (orthographic tier) that means that there is an orthographic error. This allows for classifying automatically the error at the linguistic level, that is, to assign the first letter of the tag (S, in this case). But we can go further in some cases and assign also the error code letter(s). For example, we have an error type for accentuation marks (also S at second position in the error tag). For this error type, we can compare the student form and the *nform* to check if the difference affects only accentuation marks and, in that case, assign the corresponding letters to the error code (SS). Of course, this automatic comparison cannot be performed for the most complex error types, but in many cases it will save a lot of annotation time. This is a good example of the possibilities that COPLE2 offer to apply Natural Language Processing techniques to the annotation process.

We think that the information encoded at the error level (the three tiers described plus error codes) together with all the information already encoded in the corpus (metadata, student's modifications, teacher's corrections) will allow for complex and rich linguistic queries in COPLE2. Our aim is to encode and provide as much information as possible about different aspects of the learner corpus:
- Writing process of the learner.
- Corrections made by the teacher.
- Error corrections with POS at lemma at different tiers plus error tags.
- Metadata (type of text; age; language level; etc.).
We expect that this information can be useful for researchers of different fields: General Linguistics, Language Acquisition, Foreign Language Teaching and Learning, Computer Assisted Language Learning, etc.

5 Final Remarks

COPLE2 corpus is a new learner corpus for Portuguese that encompasses written and spoken data, with a rich XML encoding. For each text included in the corpus, it contains complete metadata (information about the author and the circumstances where the text was produced) and linguistic annotation concerning POS, lemma and modifications/corrections done by the student and the teacher in the original text. Besides this, it will offer soon error-annotation, being the first learner corpus of Portuguese with this type of encoding. Error tagging is an added-value in learner corpora, since it provides valuable quantitative (error statistics) and qualitative (type of error) data that highlight the learners' difficulties. TEITOK's architecture (where each token contains all the linguistic information, following TEI) facilitates the error annotation process. Furthermore, using the CQP search functionality, error tagging information could be combined with the other linguistic features encoded in the corpus, allowing for complex and rich linguistic searches in learner texts. By combining search queries, we can easily conduct studies based on Contrastive Interlanguage Analysis (Granger, 1996, 2015), which allow for uncovering distinctive features of specific L1 learners, as well as general errors across the learner population. Finally, COPLE2 will provide different visualizations of the learner text: text produced by the student; version orthographically corrected; version grammatically corrected and version lexically corrected.

The TEITOK environment provides POS and lemma automatic annotation, along with a full set of functionalities for manual linguistic annotation, as well as visualization and powerful search options. Since it is a highly customizable tool, with a wide range of user-defined annotations, it has proven a valuable resource for corpus analysis.

We believe that this corpus and tool constitute good resources for pedagogical foreign language learning/teaching analysis, since it provides empirical data to: (i) identify general and specific errors in the learning of Portuguese L2; (ii) develop automatic tools for language learning, textbooks and other material targeting specific groups of students; (iii) implement teacher training materials; (iv) illustrate the writing-speech interaction, which has not been the subject of much analysis and has been insufficiently evaluated.

References

Boyd, A., J. Hana, L. Nicolas, D. Meurers, K. Wisniewski, A. Abel, K. Schöne, B. Štindlová and C. Vettori. 2014. The MERLIN corpus: Learner Language and the CEFR. In *Proceedings of LREC*, Reykjavik, Iceland. pp.1281--1288.

Burnard, L. and S. Bauman. Eds. 2013. *TEI P5: Guidelines for Electronic Text Encoding and Interchange*. Text Encoding Initiative Consortium: Charlottesville, Virginia.

Council of Europe. 2001. *Common European framework of reference for languages: Learning, teaching, assessment*. Cambridge, U.K: Press Syndicate of the University of Cambridge.

Cresti, E. and M. Moneglia. Eds. 2005. *C-ORAL-ROM. Integrated Reference Corpora for Spoken Romance Languages*. Amsterdam/Philadelphia: John Benjamins Publishing Company.

Christ, O., B. Schulze, A. Hofmann and E. Koenig. 1999. *The IMS Corpus Workbench: Corpus Query Processor (CQP): User's Manual*. Institute for Natural Language Processing. University of Stuttgart. (CQP V2.2).

Dagneaux, E., S. Denness, S. Granger, F. Meunier, J. Neff and J. Thewissen. Eds. 2005. *Error Tagging Manual. Version 1.2*. Centre for English Corpus Linguistics. Université Catholique de Louvain.

Delais-Roussarie E. and H. Yoo. 2010. The COREIL corpus: a learner corpus designed for studying phrasal phonology and intonation. In K. Dziubalska-Kołaczyk, M. Wrembel and M. Kul (Eds). *Proceedings of New Sound* 2010. Poznan, Pologne, pp. 100--105.

Díaz-Negrillo, A. & Fernández-Domíguez, J. 2006. Error Tagging Systems for Learner Corpora. RESLA, 19:83--102.

Granger, S. 1996. From CA to CIA and back: An integrated approach to computerized bilingual and learner corpora. In K. Aijmer, B. Altenberg and M. Johansson (Eds.). *Languages in Contrast. Text-based cross-linguistic studies*. Lund Studies in English 88. Lund: Lund University Press, pp. 37--51.

Granger, S. 2003. Error-tagged Learner Corpora and CALL: A Promising Synergy. CALICO Journal 20 (3). Special issue on error analysis and error correction in computer-assisted language learning, pp. 465--480.

Granger, S. 2004. Computer learner corpus research: current status and future prospects. In U. Connor & T. Upton (Eds.), Applied Corpus Linguistics: A Multidimensional Perspective (pp. 123-145). Amsterdam & Atlanta: Rodopi.

Granger, S. 2015. Contrastive Interlanguage Analysis: a reappraisal. *International Journal of Learner Corpus Research*. Vol. 1:1. John Benjamins Publishing Company, pp. 7--24.

Granger, S., E. Dagneaux, F. Meunier and M. Paquot. Eds. 2009. *International Corpus of Learner English*. Version 2. UCL: Presses Universitaires de Louvain.

Hinrichs, L. 2006. *Codeswitching on theWeb. English and Jamaican Creole in e-mail communication*. Amsterdam/Philadelphia: John Benjamins Publishing Company.

Janssen, M. 2012. NeoTag: a POS Tagger for Grammatical Neologism Detection. In *Proceedings of LREC 2012*, Istanbul, Turkey.

Janssen, M. 2016. TEITOK: Text-Faithful Annotated Corpora. In *Proceedings of LREC 2016*, Portorož, Slovenia.

Leiria, I. 2001. *Léxico – aquisição e ensino do Português Europeu língua não materna*. PhD Dissertation. Faculdade de Letras da Universidade de Lisboa.

Lozano, C. 2009. CEDEL2: Corpus Escrito del Español L2. In C. M. Bretones Callejas et al. (Eds). *Applied Linguistics Now: Understanding Language and Mind / La Lingüística Aplicada Hoy: Comprendiendo el Lenguaje y la Mente*. Almería: Universidad de Almería, pp. 197--212.

MacWhinney, B. 2000. *The CHILDES Project: Tools for Analyzing Talk. 3rd Edition*. Mahwah, NJ: Lawrence Erlbaum Associates.

Mendes, A., M. Généreux, I. Hendricks. 2014. *Manual for the CRPC on the CQPweb interface*. Manual 1.3. http://alfclul.clul.ul.pt/CQPweb/doc/CRPCmanual.v1_2_en.pdf.

Mendes, A., S. Antunes, M. Janssen and A. Gonçalves. 2016. The COPLE2 Corpus: a Learner Corpus for Portuguese. In *Proceedings of LREC 2016*, Portorož, Slovenia.

Meurers, D. 2015. Learner Corpora and Natural Language Processing. In S. Granger, G. Gilquin and F. Meunier (Eds.). *The Cambridge Handbook of Learner Corpus Research*. Cambridge University Press, pp. 537--566.

Nicholls, D. 2003. The Cambridge Learner Corpus – error coding and analysis for lexicography and ELT. In D. Archer, P. Rayson, A. Wilson and T. McEnery (Eds.). *Proceedings of the Corpus Linguistics 2003 Conference*. Lancaster University, pp. 572--581.

Rosen, A., J. Hana, B. Štindlová & A. Feldman 2013. Evaluating and automating the annotation of a learner corpus. Language Resources and Evaluation pp. 1--28.

Schmidt, T. 2012. EXMARaLDA and the FOLK tools – two toolsets for transcribing and annotating spoken language. In *Proceedings of the Eighth International Conference on Language Resources and Evaluation (LREC)*. Istanbul, Turkey, pp. 236--40.

Tono, Y. 2003. Learner corpora: Design, development and applications. In D. Archer, P. Rayson, A. Wilson and T. McEnery (Eds.), *Proceedings of the Corpus Linguistics 2003 Conference*. Lancaster University, pp. 800--809.

Word comprehension and multilingualism among toddlers: A study using touch screens in daycares

Laia Fibla and **Charlotte Maniel** and **Alejandrina Cristia**
Laboratoire de Sciences Cognitives et Psycholinguistique (ENS, EHESS, CNRS)
Département d'Etudes Cognitives, Ecole Normale Supérieure, PSL Research University
29, Rue d'Ulm
Paris, 75005, FRANCE
`{laia.fibla.reixachs|alecristia}@gmail.com`

Abstract

Most previous research on young infants' spoken word comprehension has focused on monolinguals. These results may not generalize to non-monolingual populations because lexical processing may be more intricate for infants exposed to more than one language. Do toddlers learning multiple languages recognize words similarly to their monolingual peers? Answering this question will require extensive efforts, to which we contribute word comprehension data collected through a procedure aiming to be both precise and ecological. French-learning toddlers (N = 38; age range 1;11-3;4) were tested in their daycare, using a French-spoken prompt-to-picture matching task implemented on a child-friendly touch screen. Our results document some differences in accuracy, but not response time or number of trials completed, among toddlers differing in the number of languages they routinely hear. Additionally, these data suggest that it is feasible to collect good quality data from multiple children tested at once in daycares, opening the path to larger-scale studies. Future research could disentangle the many factors that are often empirically confounded with monolingual versus bilingual/multilingual status.

1 Introduction

Studying language acquisition among children exposed to multiple languages is interesting for both scientific and societal reasons. As to the former, studies on bilingual and multilingual infant language development could provide answers regarding the cognitive organization of language, and further our understanding of the system underlying early language acquisition. To take one example, there is an ongoing discussion regarding the role of the quantity of input directly addressed to the child in lexical development (Shneidman and Goldin-Meadow, 2012). Children exposed to more than one language will on average hear fewer words in each than a monolingual peer - that is, provided all else is equal among the two.

However, all else is frequently *not* equal when comparing monolingual children and those routinely exposed to more than one language. To begin with, while many bi- and multi-lingual children are exposed simultaneously to more than one language from birth, for others the acquisition of their additional language(s) occurs later on, including once the first language is already well established (de Houwer, 2009). Particularly in the latter cases, hearing multiple languages is correlated with immigrant status, itself correlated with lower education and income levels – which is itself correlated with lower levels of parental speech to the child (Hoff, 2013). As a result, studying acquisition in such populations is both complicated, and particularly relevant if one would hope to strive for equality in educational opportunities (Hoff, 2013). These arguments also underline the profound societal relevance of studies on bilingual acquisition.

Setting these confounds aside for the moment, there is mounting evidence that monolinguals and non-monolinguals differ in several ways when lexical development is considered. Specifically, vocabulary sizes in monolingual preschoolers are comparable to their bilingual peers when both languages are combined together, and translation equivalents are considered only once (Pearson et al., 1997). However, when lexica are evaluated separately, bilingual children typically score lower than monolingual on vocabulary tests targeting their common language (Bialystok et al., 2010). These differences in vocabulary size could be due to a number of reasons, but by and large it appears that they emerge due to differences in input quantity: as noted previously, when exposed to several languages, bilingual children receive less input from each language than their monolingual peers (Place and Hoff, 2011). Such differences in vocabulary size have been documented with measures ranging from free production to standardized tests of lexical comprehension administered by an experimenter.

Further research suggests that bilinguals as a population vary on speed of lexical comprehension in ways that may relate to their vocabulary size. Marchman and colleagues used a looking-while-listening task, where two visual referents are presented on the screen and a spoken prompt asks for one of them (Marchman et al., 2010). Bilingual toddlers were tested in both their languages, and their parents were asked to complete a vocabulary checklist for each language. The authors document a significant correlation between speed of word recognition and vocabulary size within languages but not across them; i.e., individual variation in parental report of English vocabulary size predicted speed of recognition for English, but not Spanish, items, and *vice versa*. Since bilinguals have a smaller vocabulary than monolinguals when languages are considered separately, it appears likely that they will also be slower to recognize words. Although this contrast has not been carried out directly, comparison with other work published by the same group confirms the prediction. Whereas bilingual 30-month-olds averaged 860-870ms response times in either language, Spanish-learning monolinguals averaged 900ms when tested much earlier, at 24 months (Hurtado et al., 2008); and English-learning monolin-

guals displayed these response times even younger, at 18 months (Fernald et al., 1998).

In sum, previous research on lexical processing suggests that bilinguals are at a disadvantage compared to monolinguals. However, one recent study using a laboratory-based touch-screen test found that Canadian 2-year-olds' performance (accuracy and response time) in the common language did not differ as a function of bilingual status (Poulin-Dubois et al., 2013). It is possible that this touch-screen task is a more accurate index of children's competence, since it has been separately found to be a better predictor of later vocabulary than e.g. parental report (Friend and Keplinger, 2008). If so, other previous work may have underestimated bilinguals' lexical abilities. An alternative explanation holds that bilinguals and monolinguals in this sample may have been better matched on confounded variables, such as parental socio-economic status, than the American samples who are more commonly studied. A final alternative is that the difference does exist but is small enough to sometimes yield false negatives. Indeed, Poulin-Dubois and colleagues briefly point out that the difference is present numerically, but may not have surfaced due to limitations in statistical power. Teasing these three alternatives apart requires gathering additional data with a similar touch-screen test.

Our study sought to contribute to the general line of research documenting the relationship between word comprehension and exposure to multiple languages. For that purpose we tested monolingual, bilingual, and multilingual French toddlers *in their common language*. Our goal was not to assess global lexicon, but only to compare them on the one language they all shared. We were inspired by Friend et al. (2008)'s Computerized Comprehension Task (CCT) when developing a two-alternative prompt-to picture matching test on an iPad®, and thus followed their lead on most methodological choices (Friend and Keplinger, 2008). Most saliently, we had numerous trials sampling from three word categories (nouns, verbs, and adjectives) and three levels of difficulties (described in detail in the Methods) so that our measure was more representative of word processing in general. Unlike Friend and colleagues, we used portable technology so as to bring the test to the childrens natural environment, the daycare, a setting which may also have leveling properties by exposing all children (monolinguals and non-monolinguals) to similar experiences. By testing in three daycares located in the 13*th* neighborhood in Paris, France, we were able to assess natural variation in lexical processing in children exposed to one, two, or more languages. Although our sample for the latter case is small, we believe there is some interest in reporting on them separately due to the scarcity of research on multilinguals (Unsworth, 2013, contains a review in current state of the art on language acquisition among children exposed to more than two languages).

2 Method

2.1 Participants

Results are based on data from 38 children (monolingual n = 17; bilingual n = 13; multilingual n = 8; M age = 2;8 - that is, 2 years and 8 months, range 1;11-3;4). Twenty-five additional toddlers could not be included for various reasons (parents did not return the questionnaire for 12 children; 6 were ran on a pilot version; 3 didn't want to play with the experimenters; 1 was absent on all test days; 2 had less than 30% exposure to French). The linguistic background of the toddlers was determined through a parental questionnaire that takes into account the amount of exposure and the time period during which the child learned each language. We classified as monolingual children who heard French more than 70% of the time (i.e., other languages less than 30% of the time). Bilinguals were exposed to French and exactly one other language (English n = 5; Arabic n = 3; Mandarin Chinese n = 3; Japanese n = 2; Italian n = 1; Spanish n = 1; German n = 1; Sonink n = 1), and received these 2 languages between 30% and 70% of the time. Multilinguals were children exposed to more than two languages, generally three or four with at least 30% of French exposure (English n = 6; Hebrew n = 1; Spanish n = 2; Arabic n = 2; Chinese n = 3; Polish n = 1, Italian n = 1; Tagalog n = 1; Ilocano n = 1; Russian n = 1; Romanian n = 1; Lingala n = 1; Dutch n = 1; Wolof n = 1; Creole n = 1).

2.2 Procedure and Stimuli

During the test, each child sat next to an experimenter in a quiet environment such as the library of the daycare. The test was implemented on two ipads® covered with child-friendly protective cases (Leader Price®). Since two children were tested at a time (each accompanied by one experimenter), during the main task both child-experimenter dyads wore soundproof age-appropriate headphones, connected to their tablet via a splitter inserted through a custom-made hole, to ensure accurate sound perception and minimize interaction across dyads.

The stimuli were selected using a procedure described in more detail elsewhere (Maniel, 2016). In a nutshell, there were a total of 44 pairs of words, which included nouns (n = 23 pairs), verbs (n = 12) and adjectives (n = 9) with diverse frequencies of occurrence: high (n = 17 pairs), moderate (n = 14 pairs), low (n = 13 pairs). The frequency levels were established as a function of word occurrence in two public French corpora. Prompts were adapted to the word category; for instance, for objects they were "touche le X" *touch the X*, but for verbs "touche celui qui X" *touch the one that Xs*. Paired visual stimuli were selected to be subjectively similar in complexity and color. Pairs were also matched on the following features: masculine/feminine; singular/plural; animals/people/objects. The touch-screen test started with 3 training trials (one from each word category, all of them high frequency; responses were excluded from the analysis) followed by 41 test ones. In each, an on-screen character with a prerecorded voice provided a prompt "touche le X", that matched either the left or the right picture. A correct response resulted in the on-screen character providing positive feedback (e.g. one hears "oui, c'est ça!" *yes, thats it!* and the character jumps up and down). If the touch was to the incorrect referent, then no feedback was provided. The response time was logged from the offset of the prompt. Following the CCT, responses longer than 7s were excluded from consideration for both response time and accuracy analyses. The order of presentation of the different test pairs was pseudo-randomized to avoid having three trials of the same type in a sequence, or more than two correct responses on the same side. The child was free to stop the test early.

3 Results

Since we expected that the variances across the groups would not be equal, we decided to use non-parametric analyses. The Kruskal Wallis test was used for initial comparisons combining all three groups and, when significant, we followed up with pairwise Welch's tests. Scripts and data allowing reproducibility of these results can be downloaded from https://osf.io/u2xyc/.

We found no significant difference between the groups in terms of the number of trials completed and trials attempted (i.e., where a response was recorded before 7 s) by the child [$\chi^2(2)$ = 2.25, p = .33], although there was a numerical trend for lower numbers of trials completed for children exposed to more than one language (bilinguals com pleted 31, and attempted 29 on average; multilinguals completed 31, and attempted 28) than monolinguals (completed 35, and attempted 23).

Following criteria set in advance of data analyses, only children having produced valid responses for at least 9 trials were included for the accuracy analyses (3 children were excluded). In these accuracy analyses, results aligned with predictions made on the basis of number of languages in the input, with higher percentages of correct responses for monolinguals (monolingual, M = 86.93, SD = 13.46) than bilinguals (M = 73.86, SD = 19.31), and for the former than multilinguals (M = 67.31, SD = 16.46; see Figure 1), differences that were significant in a three-way comparison [$\chi^2(2)$ = 8.1, p = .02]. Pairwise comparisons involving monolinguals achieved significance in one-tailed Welch's tests [versus bilinguals, t(18.95) = 1.99, p = .03; versus multilinguals [t(12.11) = 2.89, p = .007]; but not that comparing bilinguals versus multilinguals [t(16.76) = 0.81, p = .21].

Response times were extracted from all correct trials, and the median was estimated for children having at least 4 valid responses, resulting in the same 35 children being included (see Figure 2). We report the median as a more accurate measure since distributions of reaction time are not normal. There were no significant differences between groups [$\chi^2(2)$ = 2.36, p = .31], with numerically shorter responses among monolinguals (Mdn = 2121 ms, SD = 379) than bilinguals (Mdn = 2461, SD =

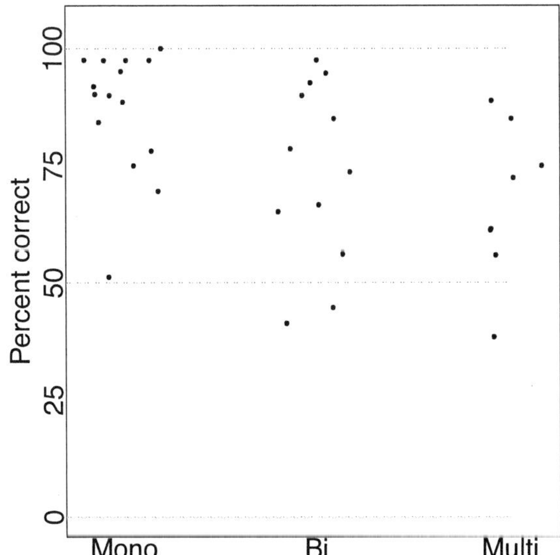

Figure 1: Accuracy as a function of language experience.

551; t(18.78) = 1.47; p = .08); multilinguals (Mdn = 2401, SD = 565) were not slower than bilinguals.

4 Discussion

We found that all three groups completed over 30 trials on average, a high number given their young age. Additionally, analyses reported elsewhere (Maniel, 2016) demonstrate that these data are sensitive to a number of individual characteristics, with strong inverse correlations between age and response time, for instance. This gave us confidence to explore the relationship between language experiences and lexical outcome measures. Our results show the same pattern as the one previous study using touch screens: Just like Poulin-Dubois et al. (2013), we find a numerical advantage whereby monolinguals have higher accuracies and faster responses than bilinguals, but the difference is not always statistically significant

The fact that some of these differences did not reach significance could be lead to three (mutually compatible) explanations. First, laboratory-testing may lead to more sensitive measures than non-laboratory testing. Second, testing toddlers on just one of their languages could narrow group differences compared to when bilingual toddlers have to complete the same test in both languages, due to interference effects. Neither of these two explanations fit current data well since they both predict greater

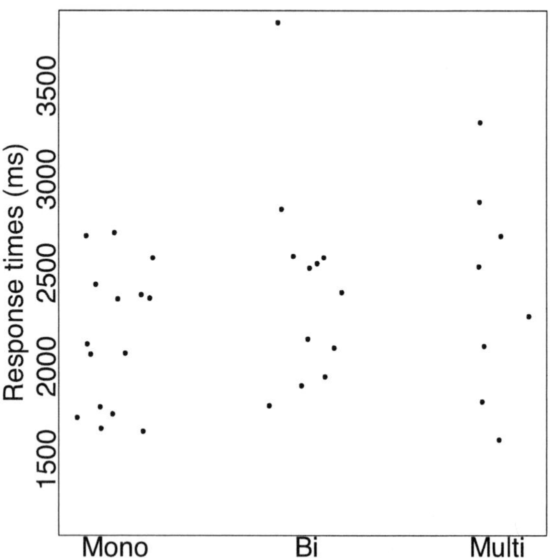

Figure 2: Response time as a function of language experience.

differences in Poulin-Dubois et al. (2013) than here because they tested bilingual children in both their languages, and they tested in the lab, unlike us – yet we obtained similar results. Third, perhaps touch-based tests are not as sensitive as other measures, because an overt motor response is required that reduces the impact of cognitive differences in processing. Only one study has been carried out comparing visual and touch-based responses, and data pertained monolingual 16-month-olds (Hendrickson et al., 2015). In this (admittedly much younger) sample, visual and haptic responses were weakly correlated ($r = .4$), but haptic responses were more strongly correlated with parental vocabulary reports than visual response times ($r = .3$ versus $r = .15$, respectively), lending no support to the contention that haptic responses are *less* sensitive to individual variation than visual responses (at least in the current procedure, with visual and auditory items that do not repeat, varied in form, etc.).

All this being said, we believe that it is premature, not to mention statistically inappropriate, to interpret numeric results as evidence for differences between the groups, or p-values above .05 as evidence for equality between groups. Instead, we contend that the use of such a portable method could allow more widespread testing, leading to the larger sample sizes that are necessary to capture effects that may be relatively subtle, and that are embedded in an intrinsically variable population. Indeed, we observed here that bilinguals tended to have larger standard deviations than their monolingual peers, in consonance with the expectation that the former population contains children growing up in a range of conditions. In future work, we intend to test more toddlers so as to increase our statistical power. This is crucial given that in our sample, as in previous work on the topic, we observe a wide range of variation in a number of key factors, such as the relative proportions in which the languages are present in the environment and caregivers' education level. Although in theory a bigger sample size could allow measurements on the impact of specific characteristics of the other languages on the common language (such as proportion of words that are cognates), we believe we would not be in an ideal position to investigate this given the astounding variability in terms of the other languages spoken (see Methods section). This kind of question would benefit from cross-lab collaborations studying bilingual and multilingual populations where the other languages are more stable, such as English-French in Canada or Quichua-Spanish in Argentina. Getting a better handle on such empirical variation is a pre-requisite to attempting a complete answer to key questions on lexical development, including in the case of children exposed to multiple languages.

Acknowledgments

We thank first and foremost the children and their families, without whose help this work would have been impossible. We are very grateful for the invaluable institutional support of the Direction de Familles et Petite Enfance of Paris, the three daycares who opened their doors to us, and Anne-Caroline Fievet at the LSCP Babylab. Our recognition also to our colleagues at the LSCP and CI-IPME, with whom we are collaborating in related research, most saliently to Celia Rosemberg, whose Spanish stimuli we adapted in the present test. The present work was supported by the Agence Nationale pour la Recherche (ANR-14-CE30-0003 MechELex, ANR-10-IDEX-0001-02 PSL*, ANR-10-LABX-0087 IEC).

References

[Bialystok et al.2010] Ellen Bialystok, Gigi Luk, Kathleen F Peets, and Sujin Yang. 2010. Receptive vocabulary differences in monolingual and bilingual children. *Bilingualism: Language and Cognition*, 13(04):525–531.

[de Houwer2009] Annick de Houwer. 2009. *Bilingual first language acquisition*. Multilingual Matters Textbook, Bristol.

[Fernald et al.1998] Anne Fernald, John P Pinto, Daniel Swingley, Amy Weinbergy, and Gerald W McRoberts. 1998. Rapid gains in speed of verbal processing by infants in the 2nd year. *Psychological Science*, 9(3):228–231.

[Friend and Keplinger2008] Margaret Friend and Melanie Keplinger. 2008. Reliability and validity of the computerized comprehension task (CCT): Data from American English and Mexican Spanish infants. *Journal of Child Language*, 35(01):77–98.

[Hendrickson et al.2015] Kristi Hendrickson, Samantha Mitsven, Diane Poulin-Dubois, Pascal Zesiger, and Margaret Friend. 2015. Looking and touching: What extant approaches reveal about the structure of early word knowledge. *Developmental Science*, 18(5):723–735.

[Hoff2013] Erika Hoff. 2013. Interpreting the early language trajectories of children from low-SES and language minority homes: Implications for closing achievement gaps. *Developmental Psychology*, 49(1):4.

[Hurtado et al.2008] Nereyda Hurtado, Virginia A Marchman, and Anne Fernald. 2008. Does input influence uptake? Links between maternal talk, processing speed and vocabulary size in Spanish-learning children. *Developmental Science*, 11(6):F31–F39.

[Maniel2016] Charlotte Maniel. 2016. Effet du statut socio-économique sur la compréhension de mots des jeunes enfants à Paris. Master's thesis, Université Pierre et Marie Curie.

[Marchman et al.2010] Virginia A Marchman, Anne Fernald, and Nereyda Hurtado. 2010. How vocabulary size in two languages relates to efficiency in spoken word recognition by young Spanish–English bilinguals. *Journal of Child Language*, 37(04):817–840.

[Pearson et al.1997] Barbara Z Pearson, Sylvia C Fernández, Vanessa Lewedeg, and D Kimbrough Oller. 1997. The relation of input factors to lexical learning by bilingual infants. *Applied Psycholinguistics*, 18(01):41–58.

[Place and Hoff2011] Silvia Place and Erika Hoff. 2011. Properties of dual language exposure that influence 2-year-olds bilingual proficiency. *Child Development*, 82(6):1834–1849.

[Poulin-Dubois et al.2013] Diane Poulin-Dubois, Ellen Bialystok, Agnes Blaye, Alexandra Polonia, and Jessica Yott. 2013. Lexical access and vocabulary development in very young bilinguals. *International Journal of Bilingualism*, 17(1):57–70.

[Shneidman and Goldin-Meadow2012] Laura A Shneidman and Susan Goldin-Meadow. 2012. Language input and acquisition in a Mayan village: How important is directed speech? *Developmental Science*, 15(5):659–673.

[Unsworth2013] Sharon Unsworth. 2013. Current issues in multilingual first language acquisition. *Annual Review of Applied Linguistics*, 33:21–50.

The Language ENvironment Analysis (LENA) System:
A Literature Review

Hillary Ganek & Alice Eriks-Brophy
Department of Speech-Language Pathology
University of Toronto
hillary.ganek@mail.utoronto.ca & a.eriks.brophy@utoronto.ca

Abstract

The Language ENvironment Analysis (LE-NA) System is a relatively new recording technology that can be used to investigate typical child language acquisition and populations with language disorders. The purpose of this paper is to familiarize language acquisition researchers and speech-language pathologists with how the LENA System is currently being used in research. The authors outline issues in peer-reviewed research based on the device. Considerations when using the LENA System are discussed.

1 Introduction

In the past, research on language acquisition involved short recordings or periods of in-person observations (Hart & Risley, 1995; Keller et al., 2007). This form of data collection could be cumbersome and required extensive time for analysis. The costs and logistics associated with these methodologies might be particularly unwieldy. The Language ENvironment Analysis (LENA) System is a new tool created to address these issues by combining a wearable audio recorder with automated vocal analysis software (LENA Research Foundation, 2014). The LENA Foundation's initial intention was to provide a device that parents could use to easily monitor the amount of language stimulation their child receives, however, the utility of such technology in the research world did not go unnoticed. In hopes of gathering the most naturalistic samples possible, researchers are currently using the LENA System to investigate various aspects of language acquisition including the effects of parent-child talk, television, bilingualism, communication disorders, and intervention among others (Christakis et al., 2009; Greenwood, Thiemann-

Bourque, Walker, Buzhardt, & Gilkerson, 2011; Marchman, Martinez, Hurtade, Gruter, & Fernald, 2016; Suskind et al., 2015; VanDam et al., 2015).

1.1 The LENA System

The LENA System's hardware includes a digital language processor (DLP) that can audio record for up to 16 hours. It measures 3-3/8" x 2-3/16" x 1/2", weighs less than two ounces, and consists of a display screen, a USB port for uploading, and two buttons for powering and recording. The processor is held in a specially designed t-shirt or vest with a pocket on the front to secure the device. The audio quality is a 16-bit channel at a 16kHz sample rate (Ford, Baer, Xu, Yapanel, & Gray, 2008). Once the recording is complete it can be uploaded to the LENA software. Recordings are stored in the software by participant, allowing repeated recordings of one participant to be saved and compared over time. Once uploaded and re-charged, the same participant or a new participant can use the DLP again without affecting the data stored in the software. The LENA System automatically segments the recordings into 12 categories including speakers, environmental sounds, and silence using Gaussian mixture models. A daylong audio file typically consists of 20,000 to 50,000 segments (VanDam et al., 2016). The software then estimates: *adult word count* (AWC), *child vocalization count* (CVC), and *conversational turn count* (CTC). The amount of background noise, electronic sounds, meaningful speech, and silence that were part of the child's listening environment are reported as percentages of the total sound present in the day and are displayed in user-friendly LENA generated graphs along with the AWC, CVC, and CTC. Additional details can be extracted using ADEX software provided by the LENA Foundation (Ford, et al., 2008; VanDam, Ambrose, & Moeller, 2012).

In addition to the raw data counts, Richards, Gilkerson, Paul, & Xu (2008) discuss the Automatic Vocalization Assessment (AVA) generated by the LENA System, which is correlated with traditional expressive language standard scores including those from the Preschool Language Scale - 4th Edition (PLS-4) (Zimmerman, Steiner, & Pond, 2002) and the Receptive-Expressive Emergent Language Test - 3rd Edition (REEL-3) (Bzoch, League, & Brown, 2003). To learn more about the LENA hardware and software, consult Ford et al. (2008) and Oller et al. (2010).

In order to establish reliability, human transcribers coded 70 full day English recordings and their results were compared with those obtained by the automated software (Xu, Yapanel, Gray, & Baer, 2008). This data was collected as part of the Natural Language Study (NLS), the LENA Foundation's normative study (Gilkerson & Richards, 2008). The LENA System correctly identified 82 and 76 percent of the segments humans coded as adult speech and child vocalizations respectively, indicating reasonable levels of agreement (Christakis et al., 2009; Warren et al., 2010; Xu et al., 2008; & Zimmerman et al., 2009). Validity has also been shown in Spanish, French, Mandarin, Korean, and Vietnamese (Canault, Le Normand, Foudil, Loundon, & Thai-Van, 2015; Ganek & Eriks-Brophy, in revision; Gilkerson et al., 2015; Pae et al., 2016; Weisleder & Fernald, 2013). Although these studies show high fidelity, recording in a child's natural environment can produce a degraded auditory signal that may negatively impact validation. Possible causes of interference might include environmental factors such as background noise, overlapping speech, and reverberation, speaker variation like pitch or voice quality, and hardware variability. Although LENA clothing has been rigorously tested, fabric sound absorption rates may also impact accuracy (Xu, Yapanel, & Gray, 2009).

2   Data Collection & Analysis

The authors undertook an extensive search for peer-reviewed studies that reported use of the LENA System. The search occurred over a four-year period (2012-2016) and included numerous databases including Medline, PsycINFO, and Google Scholar. The search term "LENA System" was most commonly used. Articles were also found through the LENA Foundation website which keeps a list of recently published papers as well as through conversations with other LENA users. Articles that dealt primarily with validation, the development of new algorithms, or that used the DLP to record but did not use the commercially available software were excluded. The primary purpose of this paper is to familiarize readers with how the LENA System is used to investigate language acquisition and disorders. Therefore, articles that focused on the LENA System itself, rather than these populations, are not included in the present discussion. Two articles were found that did not rely on the LENA software. Ota and Austin (2013) recorded for two hours pre- and post-treatment. They chose 15-minute segments coded by human coders for child turns, adult words, and conversational cohesiveness. Wang, Miller, and Cotina (2014), on the other hand, created and validated their own algorithms for identifying the type of talk in a classroom without using pre-existing LENA software.

The first author reviewed each article and extracted information regarding each study's methods and participants. Each variable was chosen through conversations with LENA users or by identifying issues that arose within the literature itself. The following is a list of the data that was reviewed:

Methods	Participants
Study Type	Number of Participants
LENA Variable	Ages
Number of Recordings	Languages
Length of Recordings	Socio-Economic Status
Time Intervals Analyzed	Additional Needs
Additional Assessments	
Additional Software	
Transcription Software	
Human Coders	

Table 1: Areas reviewed

3   Results: Methods

Thirty-eight articles were found using the criteria listed above. Below are the results from the table regarding the methods of reporting presented in LENA studies. An upcoming publication by Ganek and Eriks-Brophy will provide greater detail regarding the literature consulted in this review as well as in depth methodological analyses.

3.1 Type of Study

Studies were divided into three types: comparative studies that examined LENA results between at least two cohorts, longitudinal studies that measured children's progress over time, and cross-sectional studies that investigated children's ability at a specific point in time. Sixteen of the papers reviewed were comparative. They generally matched typically developing children to children with a communication disorder, though some compared language groups or treatment versus control groups. Eleven longitudinal studies evaluated child development over time. Both comparative and longitudinal studies measured the effects of treatment. Treatments including traditional speech therapy (Warren et al., 2010), formal established treatment programs such as Hanen's *It Takes Two to Talk* (Manolson, 1992; Weil & Middleton, 2011), and treatment associated specifically with provision of LENA feedback (Pae et al., 2016; Suskind et al., 2013). The remaining eleven cross-sectional studies often relied on a single day of recording.

3.2 LENA Variables

As mentioned above, the LENA System provides information on the adult word count (AWC), child vocalization count (CVC), conversational turn count (CTC), an automatic vocalization assessment (AVA), and background noise. Four studies used LENA ADEX software to collect additional variables such as male versus female adult speech (Johnson, Caskey, Rand, Tucker, & Vohr, 2014; Ramirez-Esparza, Garcia-Sierra, & Kuhl, 2014; Sacks et al., 2013; Warren et al., 2010). Abney, Warlaumont, Haussman, Ross, & Wallot (2014) used ADEX to identify child vocal onset times before running a custom script. However, currently published research seems to focus primarily on AWC along with CVC and CTC. Eight articles utilized information about background noise and only two focused on AVA scores.

3.3 Length of Recordings

VanDam et al. (2015) reported length of recording in total hours recorded across all participants while most reported the average number of hours/minutes each participant recorded. Full 16-hour recordings, the longest a LENA DLP can produce, were most commonly used (*M*=12.3, *SD*=3.3). The LENA System software requires recordings to be at least 10 hours long to complete a full automatic analysis. While 25 studies fell between 10 and 16 hours long, some studies asked participants to record for much shorter windows of time. In these cases, LENA analysis alone was usually not relied upon. Instead, researchers conducted their own analysis unrelated to the LENA variables, or added additional assessments.

3.4 Number of Recordings

Most of the papers recorded a single day (*M*=7.4, *SD*=11.6). Those that recorded for more than that usually did so to counteract any potential observations effects (Sacks et al., 2013) or to engage in longitudinal data collection (Weisleder & Fernald, 2013). Two papers reported the total number of recordings for all participants, while others presented the average for each individual.

3.5 Interval of Analysis

Some researchers chose to limit the amount of recording they used in analysis, often times using LENA data to govern segments of interest (ex. high CVC; Oller, 2010). Some researchers selected 5-minute segments, sometimes only looking at the first minute or 30 seconds (Jackson & Callender, 2014; Ramirez-Esparza et al., 2014). In 20 cases, however, no interval is stated. It is assumed that a full day recording (10+ hours) was used for analysis.

3.6 Additional Data and Software

LENA software is not always capable of providing all the data that researchers are looking for. Seven studies developed their own customized algorithms to locate their desired outcomes, such as vocal onset times (Abney et al., 2014; Warlaumont et al., 2010), consonant and vowel counts per utterance (Xu, Richards, & Gilkerson, 2014), pitch and speaking rate (Ko, Seidl, Cristia, Reimchen, & Soderstrom, 2015), and classroom speakers (Wang et al., 2014). Praat (Boersm & Weenink, 2013) and SALT (Miller & Chapman, 2013), widely available software programs, have also been used for analyzing speech sounds and language development (Burgess, Audet, & Harjusola, 2013; Ko, et al., 2015).

3.7 Human Transcription and Coding

The LENA System does not provide a transcription of the recordings. However, researchers frequently find it helpful to transcribe the data for analysis. While some validation studies refer to transcription software (Canault, et al., 2015; Gilkerson et al., 2015), none of the studies reviewed for this paper reported which tools were used in transcription.

About a quarter of the studies did not transcribe but instead simply coded recordings, marking pertinent information rather than providing a full transcript. Commonly coded variables included infant directed versus adult directed speech, activity, and language spoken, among others.

4 Participants

This section refers to the participants observed in each study. Please refer to the upcoming publication by Ganek and Eriks-Brophy for further detail.

4.1 Sample Size

The Natural Language Study (NLS) (Gilkerson & Richards, 2008), the LENA Foundation's normative study, included 329 participants. Seven studies used NLS data either as their primary source or as a comparative group. Studies for which new data was collected ranged from between one (Oller, 2010) and eighty-one (Wood, Diehm, & Callender, 2016) participants (M=24.9, SD=18.9).

4.2 Participant Age

The LENA System is validated from age 2 months to 48 month (Gilkerson & Richards, 2008). Twenty-five of the studies reviewed here had participants within this age range. Nine, however, expanded to five year olds and two observed children younger than two months old (Caskey, Stephens, Tucker, & Vohr, 2011; 2014), while two other studies had cohorts above the age range including older adults (Li, Vikani, Harris, & Lin, 2014; Vohr, Watson, St. Pierre, & Tucker, 2014). The expanded age ranges were dealt with by enlisting human coders, ignoring specific LENA outcomes,

and providing additional evidence that participants had language ages within the normative range.

4.3 Language Use

Expansion outside of English speaking populations has been limited. Most studies include only English speakers, though there have been five studies that have included English-Spanish bilingual children and six including monolingual Spanish speakers. There has also been one study conducted in Mandarin (Zhang et al., 2015) and one with a trilingual English-Spanish-German speaker (Oller, 2010). This study relied on a human coder rather than the LENA results, avoiding a validation issue.

4.4 Socio-Economic Status (SES)

Socio-economic status (SES) is a measure of a person's social position based on income, education, and occupation. Hart and Risley (1995) famously reported a correlation between SES, language stimulation, and language abilities. Their study, and those like it, inspired the creation of the LENA System. Even though the impact of SES on language outcomes is widely known, few of the studies reported here were able to control for it. Ten studies failed to report SES and another six reported that comparative groups were matched either to each other or to census data. Six represented a range of maternal educational levels. Nine of the studies reported that their samples skewed towards high SES participants while five others reported collecting only low SES participants. Two studies also reported an SES mismatch between comparative groups (Jackson & Callender, 2014; Wood, et al., 2016).

4.5 Populations

Most LENA System use in research has been conducted on typically developing children. However, eight studies have focused on children with autism spectrum disorder, six on hearing loss, one on Down syndrome, two on pre-term infants, and three on language delay.

4.6 Settings

Due primarily to the normed age ranges for the LENA System, most studies included recordings completed in the home. Six papers conducted recordings in a classroom setting specifically to evaluate possible differences in language stimulation in a different environment (Burgess, et al., 2013; Dykstra et al., 2012; Irvin, Hume, Boyd, McBee, & Odom, 2013; Jackson & Callendar, 2014; Soderstrom & Wittebolle, 2013; Wiggin, Gabbard, Thompson, Goberis, & Yoshinaga-Itano, 2012).

5   Discussion

LENA researchers are working to identify the best methods for integrating this new tool into the exploration of child language acquisition. Their work can help those new to the use of automated vocal analysis recognize best practices for LENA use.

When reading LENA studies, it is important to be aware of the LENA Foundation's normative study, the NLS. Almost 20 percent of the studies reviewed for this paper rely on this cohort either for primary data or comparative information. Interpreting LENA results, then, relies on the reader's understanding of the methods and participants included in the NLS. Additionally, repeatedly relying on a single data set can reduce the generalizability of research results.

To aid in the diversification of LENA data sets, a consortium of LENA researchers have recently joined forces to create Homebank, an online repository for LENA recordings (VanDam et al., 2016). The goal of this database is to provide researchers interested in advancing commercially available automated vocal analysis systems with extensive LENA data. The LENA System is capable of providing information on a variety of different aspects of a child's auditory environment, however, there are a number of features it does not capture. For example, 12 of the articles coded LENA recordings by hand for adult versus child-directed speech. Homebank encourages researchers as well as clinicians to donate data so that those interested in creating algorithms to identify variables similar to this one can do so.

At this point in time, the LENA System does not produce a transcription of the audio recording. Many researchers are still transcribing recordings by hand, which allows them to capture qualitative information like vocabulary and syntax along side quantitative data. Hart and Risley (1992), among others, found that quality of language input was as important if not more important than the quantity of language input. Without involving a significant amount of human-power, however, aspects that might characterize the quality of the interaction could be difficult to extract. Researchers and clinicians alike would appreciate reliable transcription software. Unfortunately, technology is not currently able to reach this goal. Outside of the LENA Foundation's own transcription protocol (Gilkerson, Coulter, & Richards, 2008), LENA literature rarely specifies how transcription was completed (transcriptionist training protocols, software programs utilized, etc.). Providing adequate details about transcription could allow for better replication and generalization of results in the future.

While LENA software has proven to have high fidelity; it can still make coding errors (VanDam et al., 2012). Occasionally it will mislabel a speaker. For example, a woman who raises her vocal pitch may be coded as a child (Gilkerson et al., 2015). Additionally, when two speakers are talking at the same time (overlapping talk) the LENA software discards both utterances (Warren et al., 2010; Xu et al., 2008). In busy homes with large families, discarding overlapping speech would likely underestimate the true number of interactions that occurred. Similar issues may also impact LENA results obtained in classroom settings. However, both Xu et al. (2009) and Warren et al. (2010) state that recordings of 12 hours or longer provide reliably accurate LENA results. Labeling errors caused by speaker confusion or overlapping sounds are likely to have less significance in a large data set. Recordings over multiple days may also increase accuracy (Xu et al. 2009). Longer recordings are therefore more likely to demonstrate accuracy in LENA results, while also providing representation of language over multiple activities and settings. However, shorter recordings may be more accessible for human coding or transcription of elements the software is incapable of calculating. Additionally, recordings less than 10 hours cannot be compared to normative data provided by the device, which may be helpful in language acquisition research.

LENA studies conducted in classroom settings are particularly susceptible to reduced accuracy due to interfering noise and overlapping speech. Soderstrom and Wittebolle (2013) point out, however, that a reduced AWC due to overlap may actually portray a more accurate picture of the information a young child or a child with a language disorder is able to process given the difficulties associated with listening in noise (Crandell, Smaldino, & Flexer, 2005; Newman, 2010). All of the studies in classrooms reviewed here included multiple students in each classroom. It is unclear, however, if the DLPs were worn at the same time. Future studies might consider comparing or synthesizing data taken from multiple participants at the same time and location to investigate validity.

Families recording with the LENA System at home, without supervision by the researcher, are free to turn off the device at any time, leading to variability in length. Eight studies controlled for length of recordings by looking at per hour/minute rates rather than reporting full recording results. Three others relied on the first 12 hours recorded, a measure that the LENA System provides automatically (Vohr et al., 2014; Warren et al., 2010; Zhang et al., 2015). Additionally, four studies removed periods during which the child was sleeping to control for long segments of silence (Marchman, Martinez, Hurtado, Gruter, & Fernald, 2016; Sacks et al., 2013; Suskind et al., 2013; Weisleder & Fernald, 2013). In order to obtain the most reliable results, LENA users must consider how they might control for length of recording.

Some researchers required more information than the LENA System is able to provide. Twenty-six papers engaged in a mixed methods approach, combining LENA results with other types of data including standardized language assessments, interviews, daily logs, and other technology such as Actograph (Santos-Lozano et al., 2012) and look-while-listening tasks (Fernald, Zangle, Portillo, & Marchman, 2008). Combining automated vocal analysis with other data collection methods can provide a more holistic picture of a child's language development.

Expanding the use of the LENA System to larger more diverse populations may help to increase our understanding of language acquisition. The majority of LENA studies were conducted with English speaking families in the United States. LENA data collected from families that speak languages other than English might inform our understanding of language acquisition universally. Additionally, the LENA System is only normed between 2 and 48 months old so data for children outside this range may be invalid. However, Wang et al. (2014) showed that the LENA System was accurate in identifying child speakers up to grade four. Increasing the age range for LENA use could provide information on language use across the lifespan. Future LENA research should also strive to achieve a representative range of SES groups.

Furthermore, this tool has been used with children who have a variety of communication disorders including hearing loss, autism, Down Syndrome, and language delays. Future research might consider replicating and increasing the types of communication disorders being investigated so that more families could benefit from the LENA System. It is also important to note, however, that many children with language disorders rely on visual languages and communication systems that will not be represented in LENA analysis.

6   Conclusion

Since the LENA System was first released, researchers have been exploring its possible place in identifying and describing language acquisition and language disorders. It has already provided intriguing results about the natural language environments of children from a number of different linguistic backgrounds and with a variety of communication abilities. The LENA System is also being used as an intervention tool in many countries around the world.

Nevertheless, as the field continues to expand, LENA users must consider what the device's true capabilities are. The LENA System is a remarkable tool for collecting data in a child's language environment. Understanding its strengths and weaknesses as well as the methods for its use will allow for enhanced interpretation of data contributing to the growth of the LENA System in both research and intervention settings.

Acknowledgments

The authors would like to thank the Connaught International Scholarship for Doctoral Students and the Ontario Graduate Scholarship for financial support. They played no role in the construction of this paper. The LENA Research Foundation has not provided funding to the authors.

References

Abney, D., Warlaumont, A., Haussman, A., Ross, J., & Wallot, S. (2014). Using nonlinear methods to quantify changes in infant limb movements and vocalizations. *Frontiers in Psychology*, 5(771), 1-15.

Burgess, S., Audet, L., & Harjusola-Webb, S. (2013). Quantitative and qualitative characteristics of the school and home language environments of preschool-aged children with ASD. *Journal of Communication Disorders*, 1-12.

Bzoch, K., League, R., & Brown, V. (2003). *Receptive-Expressive Emergent Language Test (3rd ed.)*. Torrance, CA: Western Psychological Services.

Canault, M., Le Normand, M., Foudil, S., Loundon, N., Thai-Van, H. (2015). Reliability of the Language ENvironment Analysis system (LENATM) in European French. *Behavior Research Methods*, DOI 10.3758/s13428-015-0634-8.

Caskey, M., Sephens, B., Tucker, R., & Vohr, B. (2014). Adult talk in the NICU with preterm infants and developmental outcomes. *Pediatrics*, 133(3), e578-e584.

Caskey, M., Stephens, B., Tucker, R., & Vohr, B. (2011). Importance of parent talk on the development of preterm infant vocalizations. Pediatrics, 128, 910-16.

Christakis, D., Gilkerson, J., Richards, J., Zimmerman, F., Garrison, M., Xu, D., Gray, S., & Yapanel, U. (2009). Audible television and decreased adult words, infant vocalizations, and conversational turns. *Archive of Pediatric & Adolescent Medicine*, 163(6), 554-58.

Crandell, C., Smaldino, J., & Flexer, C. (2005). *Soundfield amplification: Applications to speech perception and classroom acoustics* (2nd ed.) Clifton Park, NY: Thomson Delmar Learning.

Dykstra, J., Sabatos-DeVito, Irvin, D., Boyd, B., Hume, K., & Odom, S. (2012). Using the Language ENviroment Analysis (LENA) system in preschool classrooms with children with autism spectrum disorders. *Autism*, 17(5), 582-594.

Fernald, A., Zangle, R., Portillo, A., & Marchman, V. (2008). Looking while listening: Using eye-movements to monitor spoken language comprehension by infants and young children. In I. Sekerina, E.M. Fernandez, & H. Clahsen (Eds.), Developmental psycholinguistics: On-line methods in-children's language processing (pp. 97-135). Amsterdam: John Benjamins.

Ford, M., Baer, C., Xu., Yapnel, U., & Gray, S. (2008). *The LENA language environment analysis system: audio specifications of the DLP-012* (Technical Report LTR-03-2). Boulder, CO: LENA Foundation.

Ganek, H. & Eriks-Brophy, A. (in revision). A Concise Protocol for Validating Conversational Turn Count in Vietnamese.

Gilkerson, J., Coulter, K., & Richards, J. (2008). *Transcriptional analysis of the LENA natural language corpus* (Technical Report No. LTR-06-2). Boulder, CO: LENA Foundation.

Gilkerson, J. & Richards, J. (2008). *The LENA natural language study* (Technical Report LTR-02-2). Boulder, CO: LENA Foundation.

Gilkerson, J., Zhang, Y., Xu, D., Richards, J., Xu, X., Jiang, F., Harnsberger, J., & Topping, K. (2015). Evaluating LENA System performance for Chinese: A pilot study in Shanghai. *Journal of Speech, Language, and Hearing Research*, 58, 445-452.

Greenwood, C., Thiemann-Bourque, K., Walker, D., Buzhardt, J., & Gilkerson, J. (2011). Assessing children's home language environments using automatic speech recognition technology.

Hart, B. & Risley, T. (1995). *Meaningful differences in the everyday experience of young American children*. Baltimore, MD: Paul H. Brookes Publishing.

Jackson, C. & Callender, M. (2014). Enviromental considerations: Home and school comparison of Spanish-English speakers' vocalizations. Topics in Early Childhood Special Education, 34(3), 165-174.

Johnson, K., Caskey, M., Rand, K., Tucker, R., & Vohr, B. (2014). Gender differences in adult-infant communication in the first months of life. *Pediatrics*, 134(6), e1603-e1610.

Keller, H., Abels, M., Borke, J., Lamm, B., Su, Y., Wang, Y., & Lo, W. (2007). Socialization environments of Chinese and Euro-American middle-class babies: Parenting behaviors, verbal discourses and ethnotheories. *International Journal of Behavioral Development*, 31(3), 210-217.

Ko, E., Seidl, A., Cristia, A., Reimchen, M., & Soderstrom, M. (2015). Entrainment of prosody in the interaction of mothers with their young children. Journal of Child Language, 43(2), 284-309.

LENA Research Foundation. (2014). *The LENA Research Foundation*. Retrieved from http://www.lenafoundation.org/.

Li, L., Vikani, A., Harris, G., & Lin, F., (2014). Feasibility study to quantify the auditory and social environment of older adults using a digital language processor. *Otology & Neurotology*, 35(8), 1301-1305.

Manolson, A. (1992). *It takes two to talk*. Toronto, Ontario, Canada The Hanen Centre.

Marchman, V., Martinez, L., Hurtado, N., Gruter, T., & Fernald, A. (2016). Caregiver talk to young Spanish-English bilinguals: Comparing direct observation and parent-report measures of dual-language exposure. *Developmental Science*, 1-13.

Miller, J. & Chapman, R. (2003). SALT: Systematic Analysis of Language Transcripts (v. 8.0) [computer software]. Madison, WI.

Newman, R. (2010). The cocktail party effect in infants revisited: Listening to one's name in noise. *Developmental Psychology*, 41, 352-362.

Oller, D. Kimbrough (2010). All-day recordings to investigate vocabulary development: A case study of a trilingual toddler. *Communication Disorders Quarterly*, 31(4), 213- 222.

Oller, D. Kimbrough, Niyogi, P., Gray, S., Richards, J., Gilkerson, J., Xu, D., Yapanel, U., & Warren, S. (2010). Automated vocal analysis of naturalistic recordings from Children with autism, language delay, and typical development. *Proceedings of the National Academy of Sciences of the United States of America*, 107(30), 13354-13359.

Ota, C. & Austin, A. (2013). Training and mentoring: Family child care providers' use of linguistic inputs in conversations with children. *Early Childhood Research Quarterly*, 28, 972-983.

Pae, S., Yoon, H., Seol, A., Gilkerson, J., Richards, J., Ma, L., & Topping, K. (2016). Effects of feedback on parent-child language with infants and toddlers in Korea. *First Langauge*, DOI: 10.1177/0142723716649273.

Ramirez-Esparza, N., Garicia-Sierra, A., & Kuhl, P. (2014). Look who's talking: Speech style and social context in language input to infants are linked to concurrent and future speech development. *Developmental Science*, 17(6), 880-891.

Richards, J., Gilkerson, J., Paul, T., & Xu, D. (2008). *The LENA automatic vocalization assessment* (Technical Report No. LTR-08-1). Boulder, CO: LENA Research Foundation.

Sacks, C., Shay, S., Repplinger, L., Leffel, K., Sapolich, S., Suskind, E., Tannenbaum, S., & Suskind, D. (2013). Pilot testing of a parent-directed intervention (Project ASPIRE) for underserved children who are deaf or hard of hearing. *Child Language Teaching and Therapy*, 0(0), 1-12.

Santos-Lozano, A., Torres-Luque, G., Marin, P., Ruiz, J., Lucia, A., & Garatachea, N. (2012). Intermonitor variability of GT3X accelerometer. *International Journal of Sports Medicine*, 33, 994-999.

Soderstrom, M. & Wittebolle, K. (2013). When do caregivers talk? The influences of activity and time of day on caregiver speech and child vocalizations in two childcare environments. *PLoS ONE*, 8(11), e80646.

Suskind, D., Leffel, K., Graf, E., Hernandez, M., Gunderson, E., Sapolich, S., Suskind, E., Leininger, L., Goldin-Meadow, S., & Levine, S. (2015). A parent-directed language intervention for children of low socioeconomic status: A randomized controlled pilot study. Journal of Child Language, 43(2), 366-406.

Suskind, D., Leffel, K., Hernandez, M., Sapolich, S., Suskind, E., Kirkham, E., & Meehan, P. (2013). An exploratory study of "quantitative linguistic feedback": Effect of LENA feedback on adult language production. *Communication Disorders Quarterly*, 34(4), 199-209.

VanDam, M., Ambrose, S. E., & Moeller, M. P. (2012). Quantity of parental language in the home environments of hard-of-hearing 2-Year-Olds. *Journal of Deaf Studies and Deaf Education Advanced Access*, 1-19.

VanDam, M., Oller, K., Ambrose, S., Gray, S., Richards, J., Xu, D., Gilkerson, J., Silbert, N., & Moeller, M. (2015). Automated vocal analysis of children with hearing loss and their typical and atypical peers. *Ear & Hearing*, 36(4), e146-e152.

VanDam, M., Warlaumont, A., Bergelson E., Cristia A., Soderstrom M., De Palma P., and MacWhinney, B. (2016). HomeBank: An online repository of daylong child-centered audio recordings. *Seminars in Speech and Language,* 37(2), 128-141.

Vohr, B., Watson, V., St Pierre, L., & Tucker, R. (2014). The importance of language in the home for school age children with permanent hearing loss. *Acta Paediatrica,* 103(1), 62-69.

Wang, Z., Miller, K., & Cortina, K. (2014). Automatic classification of activities in classrooms discourse. *Computers and Education,* 78, 115-123.

Warlaumont, A., Oller, K., Dale, R., Richards, J., Gilkerson, J., & Xu, D. (2010). Vocal interaction dynamics of children with and without autism. *Proceedings of the 32nd Annual Conference of the Cognitive Science Society,* 121-126.

Warren, S., Gilkerson, J., Richards, J., Oller, K., Xu, D., Yapanel, U., & Gray, S. (2010). What automated vocal analysis reveals about the vocal production and language learning environment of young children with autism. *Journal of Autism Developmental Disorders,* 1-15.

Weil, L. & Middleton, L. (2011). Use of the LENA tool to evaluate the effectiveness of a parent intervention program. *Perspectives on Language Learning and Education,* 17, 108-111.

Weisleder, A. & Fernald, A. (2013). Talking to children matters early language experience strengthens processing and builds vocabulary. *Psychological Science,* 24(11), 2143-2152.

Wiggin, M., Gabbard, S., Thompson, N., Goberis, D., & Yoshinaga-Itano, C. (2012). The school to home link: summer preschool and parents. *Seminars in Speech and Language,* 33(4), 290-296.

Wood, C., Diehm, E., & Callender, M. (2016). An investigation of language environment analysis measures for Spanish-English bilingual preschoolers from migrant low-socioeconomic-status backgrounds. *Language, Speech, and Hearing Services in Schools,* 47, 123-134.

Xu, D., Richards, J., & Gilkerson, J. (2014). Automated analysis of child phonetic production using naturalistic recordings. *Journal of Speech, Language, and Hearing Research,* 57(5), 1638-1650.

Xu, D., Yapanel, U., & Gray, S. (2009). Automatic childhood autism detection by vocalization decomposition with phone-like units. *The 2nd Workshop on Child, Computer and Interaction,* 1-7.

Xu, D., Yapanel, U., Gray, S., & Baer, C. (2008). *Signal processing for young child speech language development.* Presented at The 1st Workshop of Child, Computer and Interaction, Chania, Crete, Greece.

Zhang, Y., Xu, X., Jiang, F., Gilkerson, J., Xu, D., Richards, J., Harnsberger, J., Topping, K. (2015). Effects of quantitative linguistic feedback to caregivers of young children: A pilot study in China. *Communication Disorders Quarterly,* 37(1), 16-24.

Zimmerman, F., Gilkerson, J., Richards, J., Christakis, D., Xu, D., Gray, S., & Yapanel, U. (2009). Teaching by listening: The importance of adult-child conversations to language development. *Pediatrics,* 124, 342-349.

Zimmerman, I. L., Steiner, V., & Pond, R. (2002). *Preschool Language Scale (4th ed.).* San Antonio, TX: Psychological Corp

Perception of Lexical Tones by Swedish Learners of Mandarin

Man Gao
Dalarna University
mao@du.se

Abstract

Models of cross-language perception suggest that listeners' native language plays a significant role in perceiving another language, and propose that listeners assimilate non-native speech sounds to similar sounds in their native language. In this study, the effect of native language on the perception of Mandarin tones by Swedish learners is examined. Swedish learners participated in an identification task, and their performance was analyzed in terms of accuracy percentages and error patterns. The ranking of difficulty level among the four lexical tones by Swedish listeners differs from that found among English native listeners in previous studies. The error patterns also reveal that Swedish listeners confuse Tone 1 and 2, Tone 3 and 4, and Tone 2 and 4, the first two pairs rarely being confused by English listeners. These findings may be explained with the assimilation account: Swedish learners assimilate Tone 3 and 4 to Swedish pitch accents, thus they exhibit a unique pattern when perceiving the tones in Mandarin.

1 Introduction

Recent years have witnessed a rapid growth of Chinese as a foreign language in Sweden, with an increasing number of high school students choosing to study Chinese. Two major hurdles for Swedish students wishing to learn Mandarin Chinese are the tonal system and the orthographic system, i.e. the Chinese characters. Previous studies suggest that it is difficult for learners who are not from a tone language background to acquire tones (Kiriloff 1969, Shen 1989). However, Swedish, along with a few other languages such as Japanese, have what are known as pitch accents. Pitch differences are used in more restrictive ways to contrast meaning among certain sets of words, as between *anden* 'the duck' and *anden* 'the spirit' in Swedish. Pitch accent languages are therefore often treated as being typologically intermediate between tone languages (e.g. Chinese) and non-tonal languages (e.g. English), at times even described loosely as having "another type of tone system" (McGregor 2015:346). The question whether Swedish pitch accents exert any influence on learning Mandarin tones is thus significant both from a theoretical and practical perspective (for Swedish teachers and learners). Therefore a pilot experiment was conducted to examine how Swedish learners perceive Mandarin tones and the possible influence of Swedish pitch accents.

Cross-language perception research tends to be somewhat complicated, however. There are typically multiple related factors that come into play during the process of perceiving non-native speech, and many of these additionally often interact to a great extent (Jenkins & Yeni-Komshian, 1995). For example, the listener's age, experience with the non-native target language, amount of exposure to the target language, and the degree of similarity with the native language, among many other factors, may affect how sound contrast of a non-native language is perceived (Best, 1995; Flege, 1995; Yamada, 1995). Influence of the native language on the perception of a foreign language has consistently proven to be significant across a wide range of studies (Wenk, 1986; Odlin 1989; Jenkins & Yeni-Komshian, 1995). Among the theoretical models in this field is the Perceptual Assimilation Model (PAM) (Best, 1995). In brief, it focuses on the perception of non-native speech contrasts, and hypothesizes that listeners tend to assimilate non-native speech segments to the most similar ones among their native phonetic categories. Another influential model is the Speech Learning Model (SLM) (Flege, 1995). It focuses on the learning of second languages (thus for both perception and production), and one of its suggestions is that learners relate perceptually the sounds in a second language (L2) to the most similar sounds in their first language (L1). A deeper comparison between the models is beyond the present scope. However, while PAM and SLM differ in many aspects, they make similar hypothesis in certain regards. In non-technical terms, if two languages have certain speech sounds that are highly similar, the listener will assimilate the non-native sound to the native sound category in perception. In other words, learners will make reference to the native sounds when interpreting the corresponding non-native ones if these are similar enough. This hypothesis has been tested on segmental categories across a multitude of languages (Best et al., 1988; Best & Strange, 1992; Flege, 1988; 1991; 1993; Guion et al., 2000; Polka, 1992; etc.). Thus far, however, a few studies have put them to test on prosodic categories (Hao, 2014; Reid, et al., 2015; Alexander and Wang, 2016).

A considerable amount of research has been devoted to the perception of Mandarin tones by non-native speakers. To begin with, results suggest that discriminating and identifying Mandarin tones may generally be regarded as fairly challenging for listeners from a non-tonal language background (e.g. Kiriloff, 1969; Broselow, Hurtig, Ringen, 1987; Shen, 1989; Chen, 1997; Wang et al., 1999). However, the relative degree of perceptual difficulty appears to vary across the four Mandarin tones. Several studies on speakers from a non-tonal language background have found that Tone 4 tends to be the easiest among the four to perceive correctly, and Tone 2 and Tone 3 often considerably more difficult (Kiriloff, 1969; Broselow, Hurtig & Ringen, 1987; Hao 2012). English speakers tend mainly to confuse the Tone 2-Tone 3 pair, as well as the Tone 1-Tone 4 pair (Kiriloff, 1969; Chen, 1997; So & Best, 2010; Hao, 2012). As mentioned previously, research has commonly found learners with a tonal language background to out-perform those with a non-tonal language background in various perception tasks

(Lee et al., 1996; Liang & van Heuven, 2007). Unfortunately, so far few studies have examined the performance of pitch accent language speakers on the perception of Mandarin. So and Best (2010) investigated the perception of Mandarin tones by naive listeners (having had no previous training in Mandarin) from three language backgrounds: Hong Kong Cantonese (tonal), Japanese (pitch accent) and Canadian English (non-tonal). They found that listeners with the tone language and pitch accent language backgrounds (Cantonese, Japanese) outperformed those with a non-tonal background (English). However, the predicted assimilation between certain Japanese pitch accents and Mandarin tones sharing pitch contours was not found in this study. The authors' explanation is that such mapping of similar pitch patterns across the two languages has not yet been established owing to the limited previous exposure to Mandarin tones. The current paper will report a small-scale study aiming to examine whether Swedish learners assimilate prosodic categories with similar pitch contours in Mandarin and Swedish in perception tasks.

2 Prosodic categories in Mandarin and Swedish

2.1 Mandarin tones

Mandarin Chinese has four lexical tones and an additional 'neutral' tone. Each lexical tone is carried by a monosyllable and is used to contrast lexical meaning. Table 1 below summarizes the tone system in Mandarin. Conventionally, the four tones are named Tone 1, 2, 3 and 4 respectively. Alternatively, they may be referred to by their descriptive labels, corresponding to the overall shape of their pitch contour. Tone 1 (high level) is the only level (static) tone in Mandarin; the rest are contour (dynamic) tones. The neutral tone (Table 1, bottom row), sometimes referred to as 'Tone 5', only occurs in unstressed short syllables. It does not have a stable pitch height or contour but is dependent on its tonal environment.

Tone	Example	Pinyin	Translation	Descriptive name
Tone 1	妈	mā	'mother'	(high) level
Tone 2	麻	má	'hemp'	rising
Tone 3	马	mǎ	'horse'	low/low falling-rising
Tone 4	骂	mà	'scold'	falling
Tone 5	吗	ma	'question particle'	n.a.

Table 1: Lexical tones in Mandarin (Chinese)

Figure 1 displays the pitch contours of the four tones over time, extracted from four Mandarin female speakers' production of the syllable *ma* in isolation (Burnham et al., 2015:1461). The four tones span over the pitch range from low to high. Tone 1 is a level tone that stays in the high pitch range. Tone 2 is a rising tone that rises from the mid pitch range to the high pitch target. Tone 3 is a low falling tone that reaches its low target and rises slightly at the end. Tone 4 is a falling tone that first rises to the high pitch range and then drops dramatically toward the pitch target in the lowest pitch range.

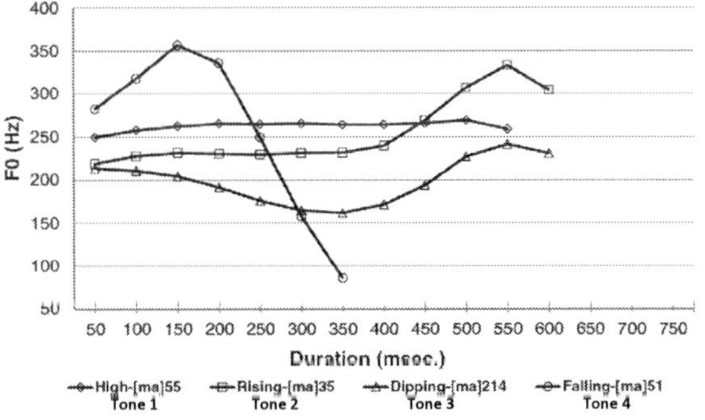

Figure 1: Pitch contours of four Mandarin tones (Burnham et al., 2015:1461).

A system based on the Scale of Five Pitch Levels (Chao 1968) is often used to represent the Mandarin tones. The pitch range in divided into five levels of relative pitch height (from 1 to 5, low to high). Tone 1 is represented as 55, which means that it starts at the highest level (5) and ends there (5). Tone 2 is characterized as 35, Tone 3 as 214 and Tone 4 as 51. An alternative characterization is offered within the framework of Autosegmental Phonology (Goldsmith, 1976). The phonological representations for Mandarin tones contain two parts: register and Tone

(Yip, 1980, 1989). In simplified terms, register in this system refers to the pitch range where a tone is realized ([-upper] for Tone 3 and [+upper] for the other three tones), and Tone specifies the direction of pitch change: H or L ([+raised] or [-raised]). Tone 1 is then represented as H, Tone 2 is LH, Tone 3 is L and Tone 4 is HL.

2.2 Swedish pitch accents

Along with Norwegian and Japanese, Swedish is labelled as a pitch accent language, or alternately a word accent language. Swedish has two pitch accents: Accent 1 ('acute') and Accent 2 ('grave'). Like lexical tones in Mandarin, they may contrast the meaning between words containing the same segmental string. Unlike lexical tones in Mandarin, however, the Swedish accents do not contrast monosyllabic words in Swedish, and Accent 2 is only seen in words with more than one syllable (Elert 1981). Various analyses argue that the distribution of the two accents may be accounted for with phonological and morphological rules (Bruce 1977, Gårding 1977, Riad 1996). There are only about 350 (Elert 1971) to 500 minimal pairs (Clark & Yallop, 1990) relying on the pitch accent contrast.

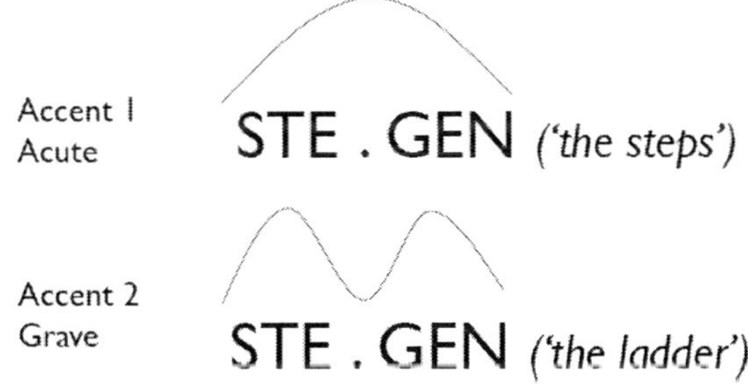

Figure 2: Schematic representation of pitch accents in Central Standard Swedish (Adopted from Engstrand 1997:62).

Figure 2 illustrates a schematic representation of the two accents in Central Standard Swedish. Accent 1 is described as a 'single falling' tone that has only one peak. Accent 2 has two peaks, reflecting primary and secondary stress respectively (Malmberg 1963).

Figure 3 displays the pitch contours of the two Swedish pitch accents over time, extracted from three female Swedish speakers' productions of disyllabic words (Burnham et al., 2015:1462). The single falling pitch contour of Accent 1 is most easily seen when the entire word is considered. For the disyllabic word carrying Accent 2, the two separate peaks are discernible by a falling contour on each of the syllables.

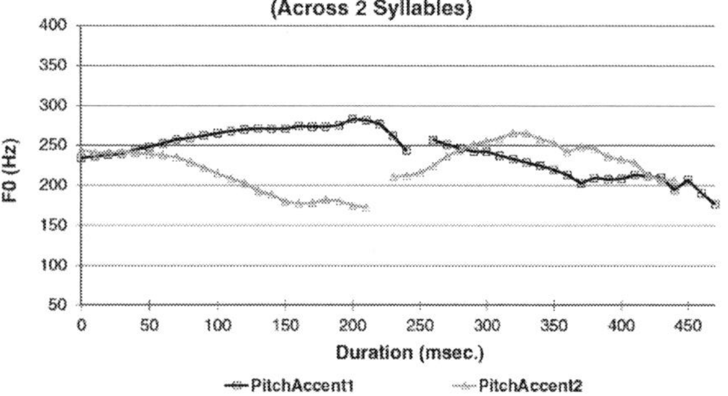

Figure 3: Pitch contours of two Swedish pitch accents (Burnham et al., 2015:1462).

Bruce (1986) proposed a phonological representation for the two Swedish pitch accents within the framework of Autosegmental Phonology (Goldsmith, 1976). He used a star notation (*) to represent the association between tone and the stressed syllable. Accent 1 is represented as HL* and Accent 2 as H*L. Bailey (1988) adopted a similar representation: HL is used to represent the single falling accent (Accent 1), and HLHL for the double peaks of Accent 2. However, he proposed that the underlying representation of the two pitch accents is the same: HL.

2.3 A comparison

Having touched upon the basic phonetic features and the phonological treatment of the prosodic systems in Mandarin and Swedish, a brief comparison between Chinese tones and Swedish pitch accents will be offered. To begin with, both languages use tonal (pitch) variations to contrast meaning, although only a subset of Swedish words rely on such contrast. Secondly, the falling pitch contour is found in both languages, as evidenced by pitch contours extracted from empirical data and phonological representations. In Swedish, disyllabic words carrying Accent 1 have the falling contour (mainly) on the second syllable, whereas disyllabic words carrying Accent 2 display two consecutive falling contours,

one on each syllable. In Mandarin Chinese, the falling contour is seen in (single) syllables carrying Tone 3 or Tone 4. Thirdly, Tone 3 and 4 differ from Swedish pitch accents in manner. For Tone 3, the falling contour is followed by a slight rise at the end, when pronounced in isolation. Tone 4 displays a very sharp fall from the highest to the lowest pitch level. The falling contour is not quite as dramatic for Tone 3, in line with its labelling as '214' in Chao's (1968) Scale of Five Pitch Levels and as 'L' in Yip's framework (1980, 1989). However, empirical data of the Swedish pitch accents (Burnham et al., 2015) clearly reveals that neither accent is associated with a dramatically falling contour when compared to the Chinese tones. Finally, Mandarin Tone 1 is a level (static) tone, a type not found in Swedish. Tone 2 has a rising tone, displaying a pitch rise throughout the carrier syllable, thus also not resembling any of the Swedish pitch accents in terms of associated pitch contour.

3 Method

16 high school students (10 Male and 6 Female) who have studied Mandarin Chinese as modern language for 3 to 4 terms participated in an identification task. They were recruited from two high schools located in Jönköping and Västra Götaland Counties respectively. Twelve (10M, 2F) students are from the school in Västra Götaland and study Chinese for 120 minutes per week; four are from the school in Jönköping and study Chinese for 180 minutes weekly. All students are native speakers of Swedish[1], and except Mandarin Chinese they all have knowledge of one or two non-tonal languages as foreign or second language (e.g. English, German). All of them were very used to reading and writing Pinyin (the Chinese phonetic alphabet).

The listening material included a total of 40 tokens of 10 different syllables: *ba, pao, fa, ge, mo, pi, tan, wan, ya* and *yi*. These syllables were chosen because they can carry all four lexical tones in Mandarin. They furthermore consist of consonants and vowels which are commonly found in other languages and were considered less challenging for the

---

[1] Though these students may speak a form of Swedish that is different from the Swedish presented in Figure 3, it has been reported in the literature (Gårding, 1977; Riad, 1996) that Swedish dialects vary mainly in terms of the timing pattern between the peak and the segmental string for both accents, and the number of peaks for Accent 2. As to the shape of corresponding pitch contours, the falling contour is seen in nearly all dialects for both Accent 1 and Accent 2 (Gårding, 1977).

students, who would thus be in a better position to focus only on the perception of tones. The tokens were presented to the Swedish learners in random order. Five monosyllables were added before these to act as fillers and warm-up items; responses to these five items were excluded from the analysis.

A female native Beijing Mandarin speaker was recruited to produce the speech material for the perception task. She was instructed to read a list of monosyllables in random order, and was recorded in an anechoic chamber. Acoustic data were collected at a sampling rate of 16 kHz with a Brüel & Kjær microphone. The distance between the speaker's mouth and the microphone was adjusted for optimal output (about 30 cm). The speech output was captured on the hard drive. The recorded speech material was subsequently reorganized using Praat (Boersma and Weenink, 2005) and presented to the Swedish learners in the form of wav format. In the perception experiment, every Swedish learner listened to the prepared listening material on a laptop using a headset and they were asked to complete a four-alternative identification task; after hearing each monosyllable, they had to select the corresponding tone on a response sheet. Participants were given six seconds to respond before being presented with the next token. The decision time for a similar task was reported to be less than four seconds (So and Best, 2010).

4 Results

The students' performance in the perception task is summarized in figure 4. Accuracy percentages were calculated separately for the two schools. Students from the school in Jönköping overall performed significantly better than those from Västra Götaland, with the former scoring between 65% and 95% and the latter 37.5% to 80%. Significantly, however, both groups presented the same pattern in terms of the relative level of difficult among the four Mandarin tones. For that reason the results for both groups will be pooled in the following analysis.

The students' accuracy rates indicate that Tone 3 is the easiest to identify, followed by Tone 4, then Tone 1, and, finally, with Tone 2 being the most difficult. Paired samples t-tests show that only the accuracy rates for Tone 3 and Tone 4 are not signifi-

cantly different (p=0.315); all the other combinations are different at the level of p=0.020 (for Tone 1 and 3 pair, and Tone 1 and 4 pair) or p=0.000.

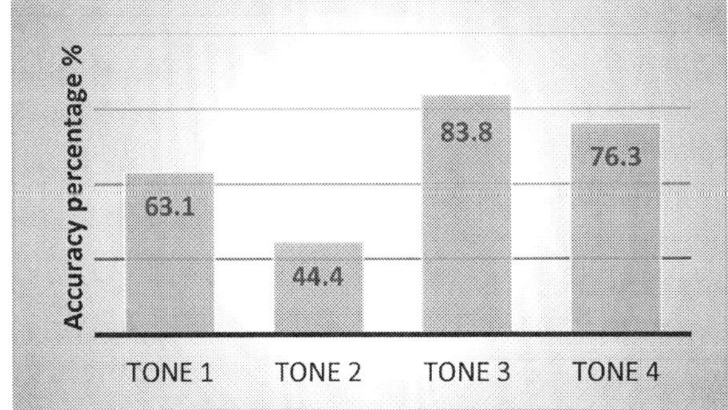

Figure 4: Accuracy percentage of identification task.

The error patterns for the identification task were also analyzed and compared. Table 2 displays the error matrix, in which the top row represents listeners' answers and the first column corresponds to the actual tone. Tone 1 is most likely to be misperceived as Tone 2 and vice versa. Tone 3 is most likely to be misperceived as Tone 4, but not vice versa; rather Tone 4 tokens, like Tone 1, are most likely to be misidentified as Tone 2. Some listeners were unable to identify a small number of tokens, most of which being Tone 2 syllables.

Response Target	Tone 1	Tone 2	Tone 3	Tone 4	unable to iden- tify
Tone 1	**63.1%**	27.5%	0.6%	8.1%	0.6%
Tone 2	23.8%	**44.4%**	13.1%	16.3%	2.5%
Tone 3	3.8%	4.4%	**83.8%**	7.5%	0.6%
Tone 4	3.8%	19.4%	0.6%	**76.3%**	0

Table 2: Lexical tones in Mandarin (Chinese)

In sum, Swedish students mainly display confusion among the following tone pairs: Tone 1 and 2, Tone 3 and 4, and Tone 2 and 4.

5 Discussion

Results of the identification task show that the relatively level of difficulty among the four lexical tones for Swedish learners is: Tone 2, Tone 1, Tone 4 and Tone 3, from most to least difficult. In comparison, for English learners Tone 3 and Tone 2 are more difficult to perceive than Tone 1 and Tone 4, according to previous results[2] (Kiriloff, 1969; Broselow, Hurtig & Ringen, 1987; Hao 2012, 2014). The assimilation hypothesis from both PAM (Best, 1995) and SLM (Flege, 1995) may be used to account for this finding. Comparison of the Mandarin and Swedish prosody systems in section 2 above suggests that Tone 3 and 4 both exhibit falling contours that resemble Swedish Accent 1 and 2. It is thus possible that Swedish learners assimilate Tone 3 and Tone 4 in Mandarin to Swedish Accent 1 and 2. Although Tone 3 receives the highest accuracy rate among the four tones, it is not significantly higher than the accuracy rate for Tone 4. The accuracy rates for the other two tones, Tone 1 and Tone 2, on the other hand, are found to be significantly lower than Tone 3 and Tone 4. Following the same line of reasoning, this may be because they cannot map them onto any prosodic categories in Swedish. This is consistent with findings from Hao's (2014) study: native English learners considered Tone 3 the least English-like lexical tone through an English-likeness rating task, and also perceived Tone 3 with the lowest accuracy rate in the identification task.

Analysis of Swedish learners' error patterns lends additional support to the assimilation account. The most commonly reported confusions for native English speakers, namely those among Tone 2 and 3 and between Tone 1 and 4 (Kiriloff, 1969; Chen, 1997; So & Best, 2010; Hao, 2012), were not found for the Swedish students. Since Swedish as a pitch accent language differs from English as a non-tonal language, it is maybe the case that Swedish influences the perception of Mandarin tones in a different manner. For Swedish speakers, Tone 3 and Tone 4 are more similar to the pitch accents and to each other, and thus not difficult to differentiate from Tone 1 and Tone 2 (this is especially true to Tone 3). The error patterns found in this study reveal that Tone 1 and Tone 2 pair is most problematic for Swedish learners. Tone 1 is nearly exclusively misperceived as Tone 2, and majority of misperceived Tone 2 tokens were labelled as Tone 1. However, there is certain proportion of Tone 2 tokens misperceived as Tone 3 or Tone 4. In combined with the accuracy rates reported in Figure 4, we may conclude here that the rising tone (Tone 2) is most challenging for Swedish learners. Another source of confusion for Swedes is the Tone 2 and Tone 4 pair, which is rarely found among native English speakers in the literature (Kiriloff, 1969; Chen, 1997; So & Best, 2010; Hao, 2012). Maybe this is because Tone 2 and Tone 4 share some similarities in terms of pitch type (both are contour tones) and pitch height (Tone 2 and part of Tone 4 are active in the mid to high pitch range), which confuse Swedish listeners. But in order to verify this explanation, further research that examines Swedish speakers' strategy (i.e. perceptual cues) when perceiving tones is recommended.

The two groups of learners, both of whom had studied Mandarin for 3 or 4 terms prior to the investigation, performed quite differently in this study. Several factors may be contributing to this. One concerns the amount of exposure to the target language (Mandarin). The Jönköping students studied approximately 60 minutes more each week than those students from Västra Götaland whom they outperformed. Second, brief and informal interviews with the two instructors indicate that they may have quite different teaching style. The teacher from Jönköping stated that she tried to speak as much Mandarin as possible in class, and put a lot of emphasis on improving students' spoken proficiency. The second teacher seemed to place a lot of emphasis on vocabulary and grammar, and to be speaking mostly Swedish to his students. Therefore, the differences between the two school students in the perception task may stem from their different proficiency level in Mandarin, especially regarding spoken proficiency

6   Conclusion

The current study is the first attempt to investigate whether Swedish learners assimilate Mandarin tones to Swedish pitch accents in perception. It first provided a brief overview of the prosody systems in Mandarin Chinese and Swedish. Tone 3 and 4 in Mandarin along with Accent 1 and 2 in Swedish

---

[2] A direct comparison between the Swedish learners' and English learners' performance cannot be made in this study for two reasons. One is that the raw data from previous studies is not available, thus it is impossible to apply any statistical test to verify any observed differences. Secondly, though the current study employed similar experimental design as the previous research, other factors may differ, such as participants' Chinese proficiency level and the speech material used in the listening tasks, etc. It is highly recommend to conduct a future study that compares the error patterns from matched groups of Swedish and English speakers using the same listening materials.

have a falling contour; they also receive similar phonological representation. According to the two cross-language perception models PAM and SLM, the non-native listeners are expected to assimilate the non-native sound to the closest native sound category in perception. Two groups of Swedish learners participated into a Mandarin tone identification task. The results showed that they could identify Tone 3 and 4 with a higher degree of accuracy than the other two tones, which is consistent with the assimilation hypotheses in both PAM and SLM models. Furthermore, analysis of the error patterns provided additional support for the assimilations hypothesis. This study therefore constitutes an attempt to extend the PAM and SLM models to prosodic categories, and also revealed possible clues regarding the effect of Swedish pitch accents on learners' perception of Mandarin tones. Further research is clearly needed, however, especially into (1) assessing the perceptual similarity between Mandarin tones and Swedish pitch accents; and (2) analyzing Swedish learners' production of Mandarin tones for a complete understanding of the acquisition of Mandarin tones by Swedish learners.

Acknowledgments

I would like to thank the Swedish students who participated in this study and their teachers who helped me to collect the data.

References

Jennifer Alexander and Yue Wang. 2016. Cross language Lexical-tone Identification. In *Proceedings of the 5th International Symposium on Tonal Aspects of Languages (TAL 2016)*, 28-32. New York.

Leslie M. Bailey. 1988. A Non-linear analysis of Pitch Accent in Swedish. *Linguist*, 75:103-204.

Catherine T. Best. 1995. A direct realist view of cross-language speech perception. In Winifred Strange (ed.), *Speech Perception and Linguistic Experience: Issues in Cross-Language Research*. Timonium, MD: York Press. pp.171–204.

Catherine T. Best, Gerald W. McRoberts, and Nomathemba M. Sithole. 1988. Examination of perceptual reorganization for nonnative speech contrasts: Zulu click discrimination by English-speaking adults and infants. *Journal of Experimental Psychology: Human Perception and Performance*, 4:45-60.

Catherine T. Best and Winifreed Strange. 1992. Effects of phonological and phonetics factors on cross language speech perception on approximants. *Journal of phonetics*, 20:305-330.

Paul Boersma and David Weenink. 2005. Praat: doing phonetics by computer (Version 5.1.15). Retrieved from http://www.praat.org/.

Ellen Broselow, Richard R. Hurtig, and Catherine Ringen. 1987. The perception of second language prosody. In G. Ioup and S.H. Weinberger (eds.), *Interlanguage Phonology: The Acquisition of Second Language Sound System*. Cambridge, Newbury House Publishers. pp. 350-361.

Gösta Bruce. 1977, *Swedish Word Accents in Sentence Perspective*. Lund: Gleerup.

Gösta Bruce. 1986. How floating is focal accent? In K. Gregersen and H. Bosbøll (eds.), *Nordic prosody IV*. Odense University Press. pp. 41–49.

Denis Burnham, Benjawan Kasisopa, Amanda Reid, Sudaporn Luksaneeyanawin, Francisco Lacerda, Virginia Attina, Nan Xu Rattanasone, Iris-Corinna Schwarz and Diane Webster. 2015. Universality and language-specific experience in the perception of lexical tone and pitch. *Applied Psycholingustics*, 366: 1450-1491.

Yuen Ren Chao. 1968. *A Grammar of Spoken Chinese*. Berkeley: University of California Press.

Qinghai Chen. 1997. Toward a sequential approach for tonal error analysis. *Journal of the Chinese Language Teachers Association*, 32:21–39.

John Clark and Colin Yallop. 1990. *An introduction to phonetics and Phonology*. Oxford: Basil Blackwell.

Claes-Christian Elert. 1971. *Tonality in Swedish: Rules and a List of Minimal Pairs*. Umeå: Umeå University Department of Phonetics.

Claes-Christian Elert. 1981. Ljud och ord i svenskan 2. Acta Universitatis Umensis, *Umeå Studies in the Humanities*, vol. 40. Stockholm: Almqvist and Wiksell International.

Olle Engstrand. 1997. Phonetic interpretation of the word accent contrast in Swedish: evidence from spontaneous speech. *Phonetica*, 54:61–75.

James Emil Flege. 1988. Factors affecting degree of perceived foreign accent in English sentences. *Journal of the Acoustical Society of America*, 84:70-79.

James Emil Flege. 1991. The interlingual identification of Spanish and English vowels: orthographic evidence. *The Quarterly Journal of Experimental Psychology*, 43A(3):701-731.

James Emil Flege. 1993. Production and perception of a novel, second-language phonetic contrast. *Journal of the Acoustical Society of America*, 93:1589-1608.

James Emil Flege. 1995. Second language speech learning: Theory, findings, and problems. In Winifred Strange (ed.), *Speech Perception and Linguistic Experience: Issues in Cross-language Research*. Timonium, MD: York Press. pp.233–277.

John Goldsmith. 1976. *Autosegmental Phonology*. MIT dissertation.

Susan G. Guion, James Emil Flege, Rieko Akahane Yamada, and Jesica C. Pruitt. 2000. An investigation of current models of second language speech perception: The case of Japanese adults' perception of English consonants. *Journal of the Acoustical Society of America*, 1075:2711–2724.

Eva Gårding. 1977. *The Scandinavian word accents*. Lund: Gleerup.

Yen-Chen Hao. 2012. Second language acquisition of Mandarin Chinese tones by tonal and non-tonal language speakers. *Journal of Phonetics*, 40:269–279.

Yen-Chen Hao. 2014. The Application of the Speech Learning Model to the L2 Acquisition of Mandarin Tones. In *Proceedings of the 4th International Symposium on Tonal Aspects of Languages (TAL 2014)*, 67-70. Nijmegen.

James J. Jenkins and Grace H. Yeni-Komshian. 1995. Cross-language speech perception: perspective and promise. In Winifred Strange (ed.), *Speech Perception and Linguistic Experience: Issues in Cross-Language Research*. Timonium, MD: York Press. pp.433–463.

Constantine Kiriloff. 1969. On the auditory perception of tones in Mandarin. *Phonetica*, 20:63–67.

Yuh-Shiow Lee, Douglas A. Vakoch, and Lee H. Wurm. 1996. Tone perception in Cantonese and Mandarin: A cross linguistic comparison. *Journal of Psycholinguistic Research*, 25:527–542.

Jie Liang and Vincent J. van Heuven. 2007. Chinese tone and intonation perceived by L1 and L2 listeners. In Carlos Gussenhoven and Tomas Riad (eds.), *Tones and tunes. Volume 2: Experimental studies in word and sentence prosody*. Berlin: Mouton de Gruyter. pp.27-61.

William Bill McGregor. 2015. *Linguistics: An Introduction*. New York: Bloomsbury Academic.

Bertil Malmberg. 1963. *Phonetics*. New Yorker: Dover Publications.

Terence Odlin. 1989. *Language Transfer: Cross-linguistic Influence in Language Learning*. Cambridge: Cambridge University Press.

Linda Polka. 1992. Characterizing the influence of native language experience on adult speech perception. *Perception and Psychophysics*, 521:37–52.

Amanda Reid, Denis Burnham, Benjawan Kasisopa, et al. 2015. Perceptual assimilation of lexical tone: the roles of language experience and visual information. Atten Percept Psychophys. 77(2):571-591.

Tomas Riad. 1996. Remarks on the Scandinavian Tone Accent Typology. *Nordlyd: Tromsø University Working Papers on Language and Linguistics*, 24:129–156.

Xiaonan Susan Shen. 1989. Toward a register approach in teaching Mandarin tones. *Journal of the Chinese Language Teachers Association*, 243:27–48.

Connie K. So and Catherine T. Best. 2010. Cross-language Perception of Non-native Tonal Contrasts: Effects of Native Phonological and Phonetic Influences. *Language and Speech*, 532:273-293.

Yue Wang, Michelle M. Spence, Allard Jongman, and Joan A. Sereno. 1999. Training American listeners to perceive Mandarin tones. *Journal of the Acoustical Society of America*, 1066:3649–3658.

Brian J. Wenk. 1986. Crosslinguistic influence in second language phonology: Speech rhythms. In Kellerman, E. and M. Sharwood Smith (eds.), *Crosslinguistic Influence in Second Language Acquisition*. New York: Pergamon Press. pp.120–133.

Reiko Akahane Yamada. 1995. Age and acquisition of second language speech sounds: perception of American English /r/ and /l/ by native speakers of Japanese. In Winifred Strange (ed.), *Speech Perception and Linguistic Experience: Issues in Cross-Language Research*. Timonium, MD: York Press. pp.305–320.

Moira Yip. 1980. *The Tonal Phonology of Chinese*. Cambridge, MA: The MIT Press.

Moira Yip. 1989. Contour tones. *Phonology*, 6:149-174.

Language-independent exploration of repetition and variation in longitudinal child-directed speech: a tool and resources

Gintarė Grigonytė and Kristina Nilsson Björkenstam
Department of Linguistics
Stockholm University
SE-106 91 Stockholm, Sweden
`gintare@ling.su.se`, `kristina.nilsson@ling.su.se`

Abstract

We present a language-independent tool, called *Varseta*, for extracting variation sets in child-directed speech. This tool is evaluated against a gold standard corpus annotated with variation sets, MINGLE-3-VS, and used to explore variation sets in 26 languages[1] in CHILDES-26-VS, a comparable corpus derived from the CHILDES database. The tool and the resources are freely available for research.[2]

1 Introduction

Repetitiousness is a strong trait of child-directed speech. When parents speak to young infants, a large proportion of utterances are either exact repetitions of an immediately preceding utterance, or partial repetitions, where the message is repeated and thus, the speaker intent is constant, but variation occurs in the surface form. Such sequences of partial repetitions were first referred to as *variation sets* by Küntay and Slobin (1996). Surface form variation includes expansion, insertion, deletion, and word order change, e.g.:

> *le petit chat?* ('the small cat?')[3]
> *tu m'aides?* ('will you help me?')

tu m'aides à chercher? ('will you help me look?')
il est où là le petit chat? ('where is the small cat?')

The repetitiousness can also be semantic, e.g., in cases of lexical substitution such as this where the verbs *titta, sett, kolla* are variations of 'to look (at something)' (Wirén et al., 2016):

> *titta här då!* ('look at this!')[4]
> *har du sett vilka tjusiga byxor?* ('have you seen such fancy pants?')
> *kolla!* ('check it out!')

Current research suggests that such sequences of repetition and variation play a role in language learning, e.g., experiments on artificial language learning and variation sets (Onnis et al., 2008), as well as child corpus studies on correlations between variation sets and language acquisition (Hoff-Ginsberg, 1986; Hoff-Ginsberg, 1990; Waterfall, 2006; Küntay and Slobin, 1996). This paper builds upon these assumptions, but does not concern the output of the learner. Rather, our aim is to investigate the input to the learner, and more specifically, the longitudinal patterns of occurrences of variation sets in child-directed speech across multiple languages.

To our knowledge, variation sets have been studied in Turkish (Küntay and Slobin, 1996; Küntay and Slobin, 2002), English (Waterfall, 2006), Sign Language of the Netherlands (Hoiting and Slobin,

---

[1]Afrikaans, Cantonese, Catalan, Chinese, Croatian, Danish, Dutch, English, Estonian, Farsi, French, German, Greek, Hebrew, Hungarian, Indonesian, Irish, Italian, Japanese, Portuguese, Russian, Spanish, Tamil, Thai, Turkish, Welsh.

[2]URL https://github.com/ginta-re/Varseta

[3]Example from CHILDES FrenchGeneva14.cha, PID: 11312c-00028164-1. English translations are approximate.

[4]Example from (Wirén et al., 2016). English translations are approximate.

2002), and Swedish, English, Russian, and Croatian (Wirén et al., 2016). Studies using longitudinal data have shown that as the communication skills of the child increase, the proportion of utterances in variation sets decreases (Waterfall et al., 2010; Wirén et al., 2016).

This study expands the scope of previous work by using a large-scale cross-language approach to explore repetition and variation in child-directed speech. Further, the approach proposed in this paper on extracting variation sets from transcripts of child-directed speech is language-independent and automatic. This paper presents two surface-based strategies for automatic variation detection (see section 4). The strategies are evaluated against a gold standard corpus annotated according to the annotation scheme for variation sets described in (Wirén et al., 2016).

2 Related work

While most definitions of variation sets include both speaker intention and utterance form (c.f., (Küntay and Slobin, 1996; Küntay and Slobin, 2002; Waterfall, 2006; Wirén et al., 2016)), previous attempts at automatic extraction of variation sets focus primarily on form.

Brodsky et al. (2007) suggest a narrower definition of variation set as sequences of utterances where each successive pair of utterances has a lexical overlap of at least one element. Variation sets can thus be extracted by comparing pairs of successive utterances for repeated words, resulting in sets with at least one word in common. Using such an extraction procedure, Brodsky et al. found that 21.5% of the words in Waterfall's (2006) corpus (12 mother–child dyads, child age 1;2-2;6 years) occur in variation sets, and 18.3% of the words in the English CHILDES database (MacWhinney, 2000).

Similarly, Onnis et al. based their extraction strategy on Waterfall's (2006) criteria for variation sets. When applied to the CHILDES Lara corpus (child age 1;9–3;3 years), 27,9% of the utterances were extracted as belonging to variation sets.

Also using a surface-based algorithm for automatic extraction of variation sets, but with a novel definition of variation sets, Wirén et al. (2016) show that the proportion of variation sets in child-directed speech decreases consistently as a function of children's age across Swedish, Croatian, English and Russian. They report fuzzy F-scores of 0.822, 0.689, 0.601, and 0.425 for 4 age groups in Swedish data respectively.

This study expands the scope of the latter paper in two ways: a) by offering two variation set extraction strategies ANCHOR and INCREMENTAL which are evaluated against a gold standard corpus of Swedish; b) by using these strategies in a large-scale cross-language investigation of child-directed speech corpora derived from the CHILDES database (MacWhinney, 2000); c) by releasing the software and the derived corpora along with the gold standard corpus of Swedish.[5]

3 Data sets

We use two different data sets for exploration of repetition and variation in child-directed speech. The longitudinal Swedish corpus, MINGLE-3-VS, is annotated with variation sets. The second data set, here called CHILDES-26-VS, consists of plain text transcripts of child-directed speech in 26 languages, derived from the CHILDES database (MacWhinney, 2000). The corpus files are grouped by language and child age which allows for both cross-language and within-language longitudinal comparisons.

3.1 MINGLE-3-VS: a corpus annotated with variation sets

The gold standard variation set corpus, MINGLE-3-VS, consist of transcripts of Swedish child-directed speech annotated with variation sets according to the annotation scheme described in (Wirén et al., 2016).

The transcripts originates from the MINGLE-3 multimodal corpus (Björkenstam et al., 2016), which consists of 18 longitudinal dyads with three children (two girls, one boy; six dyads per child) recorded between the ages of 7 and 33 months. The complete duration of the 18 dyads is 7:29 hours (mean duration 24:58 minutes). The video and audio recordings were made from naturalistic parent–child interaction in a studio at the Phonetics Laboratory at Stockholm University (Lacerda, 2009). The children were interacting alternately with their mothers (10 dyads) and fathers (8 dyads) in a free play sce-

---

[5]URL https://github.com/ginta-re/Varseta

CHILDES language group	Language	Corpora	# Children	Age span	# Dyads
Celtic	Irish	Gaeltacht	1	3,4	2
	Welsh	CIG1	1	3,4	2
EastAsian	Cantonese	HKU, LeeWongLeung	2	3,4	3
	Chinese	Beijing, XuMinChen, Zhou1	7	2,3,4	7
	Indonesian	Jakarta	2	3,4	2
	Japanese	Ishii, Miyata	2	1,2,3,4	6
	Thai	CRSLP	1	1,2,3,4	4
Germanic	Afrikaans	VanDulm	2	3,4	4
	Danish	Plunkett	2	1,2,3,4	5
	Dutch	Groningen, VanKampen	2	3,4	4
	English UK	Lara	1	3,4	2
	German	Caroline, Manuela, Szagun	4	1,2,3,4	9
Romance	Catalan	Julia	1	3,4	2
	French	Geneva, Hunkeler, Lyon, Pauline	4	1,2,3,4	8
	Italian	Antelmi, Calambrone	2	3,4	3
	Portuguese	Santos	2	3,4	2
	Spanish	Irene	1	1,2,3,4	4
Slavic	Croatian	Kovacevic	1	1,2,3	3
	Russian	Protassova	1	3,4	2
Other	Estonian	Argus, Kapanen, Kohler, Zupping	5	1,2,3,4	7
	Farsi	Samadi	2	3,4	2
	Greek	Stephany	1	3,4	2
	Hebrew	BSF, Levy, Naama	4	2,3,4	4
	Hungarian	Bodor, MacWhinney, Reger	3	3,4	3
	Tamil	Narasimhan	1	1,2,3,4	4
	Turkish	Aksu, Turkay	2	3,4	4
Total	26 languages	45 corpora	60	–	100

Table 1: CHILDES-26-VS: Corpora derived from the CHILDES database (MacWhinney, 2000) grouped by CHILDES language group, and presented per language. Col. 3: corpus name(s), col. 4: total number of children, col. 5: the age groups covered (1–4), col. 6: the total number of dyads.

nario.[6] The ELAN annotation tool (Wittenburg et al., 2006) was used for transcription of parent and child utterances, as well as non-verbal annotation (Björkenstam et al., 2016).

ELAN was also used for manual variation set annotation. This allowed for the annotators to take both verbal and non-verbal input from parent and child into account when deciding on the boundaries of variation sets. The annotation methodology was as follows: during the first phase, a subset of four dyads was annotated by two coders independently. After merging the respective annotations for each dyad, a third annotator marked cases of disagreement. This resulted in an inter-annotator agreement (measured as set overlap between annotators) of 78%. Disagreements were solved during group discussions. After evaluation of the first phase, the remaining 14 dyads were annotated by one annotator. Finally, a classification of communicative intention based on the Inventory of Communicative Acts-Abridged (Ninio et al., 1994) was added. This classification was evaluated by comparing four representative dyads annotated by three independent annotators, resulting in a Fleiss's kappa of 0.63. The transcripts were also annotated with part-of-speech using Stagger (Östling, 2013), followed by manual

---

[6]A subset of the audio files is available through CHILDES/Swedish/Lacerda (MacWhinney, 2000).

correction (Wirén et al., 2016).

3.2 CHILDES-26-VS: corpora derived from CHILDES

We have extracted child-directed speech from transcripts in 45 corpora in 26 languages from the CHILDES database (MacWhinney, 2000). The selection criteria was the scenario (naturalistic interaction), the participants (parents or other adults - including researchers - and children), and the age of the child (0;6 to 2;9 years). The selected transcripts were grouped according to child age. The grouping approximates major physical child development stages, i.e., sitting up (0;6–0;11 years), standing-walking (1;0–1;3 years), fully mobile (1;4–1;11 years), and talking (2;0–2;9 years) (see table 2).

	MINGLE-3-VS	CHILDES-26-VS
Age group 1	0;6 – 0;9	0;6 – 0;11
Age group 2	1;0 – 1;2	1;0 – 1;3
Age group 3	1;4 – 1;7	1;4 – 1;11
Age group 4	2;3 – 2;9	2;0 – 2;9

Table 2: Age groups and age spans (year;months) in MINGLE-3-VS and the derived corpora CHILDES-26-VS.

An overview of the sources is presented in table 1, detailing for each language the language group according to CHILDES, the name of the corpus or corpora, the total number of children, the age groups (1–4) covered by the transcripts, and the total number of transcripts.

All files in the derived corpora are grouped by language and child age which allows for both cross-language and within-language longitudinal comparisons of variation sets with the Varseta tool. This data set is freely available for research as part of the Varseta package (see section 4).

4 Varseta - a tool for automatic extraction of variation sets

The Varseta tool for variation set extraction for any language is available at GitHub[7].

The definition of variation sets that we follow in the implementation of the Varseta tool takes into account exact repetitions, and further allows the following transformations between utterances: reduc-

tion, expansion, and word order change (Wirén et al., 2016). Although these alternations might be fairly complex, a large proportion of them can be observed on the surface level, and thus automatically extracted on the basis of string similarity techniques.

Varseta employs two commonly used string similarity measures: the Ratcliff-Obershelp pattern recognition method (Black, 2004) and edit distance ratio[8] (Levenshtein, 1966), and uses two strategies for detecting variation sets in child-directed speech: ANCHOR and INCREMENTAL. The two string similarity measures and the two strategies can be used in any combination, allowing for 4 different settings.

For a given set of utterances, the ANCHOR strategy measures pairwise utterance similarity of all utterances in relation to the first, e.g. 1-2, 1-3, 1-4. The criterion for including two utterances in a variation set is that the difference between them (regarded as strings) does not fall below a certain similarity threshold. Additionally, following Brodsky et al. (2007), we allow for sequences of maximally two intervening dissimilar utterances that do not obey this condition.

For a given set of utterances, the INCREMENTAL strategy performs a stepwise comparison of pairs of successive utterances, e.g. 1-2, 2-3, 3-4. Two utterance strings that pass a certain similarity threshold are marked as belonging to a variation set. Unlike the ANCHOR strategy, sequences of intervening dissimilar utterances are not allowed. Thus the process continues, by adding similar utterances, until a non-similar utterance occurs.

Both strategies can employ either edit distance ratio (**EDR**) or Ratcliff-Obershelp pattern recognition method (**DLR**, as implemented in the Python module difflib[9]). String similarity measures return values between [0..1], convenient for categorizing string utterances on the surface level. A value of 1 means exact repetition of an utterance, and 0 means two unrelated utterances without any overlap of words. The similarity threshold used in this experimental study, as described in section 5, was arbitrarily selected. The most optimal similarity thresholds when evaluated against the Swedish gold stan-

---

[7]https://github.com/ginta-re/Varseta

[8]Also known as Levenshtein distance.

[9]difflib: https://docs.python.org/2/library/difflib.htmlmodule-difflib

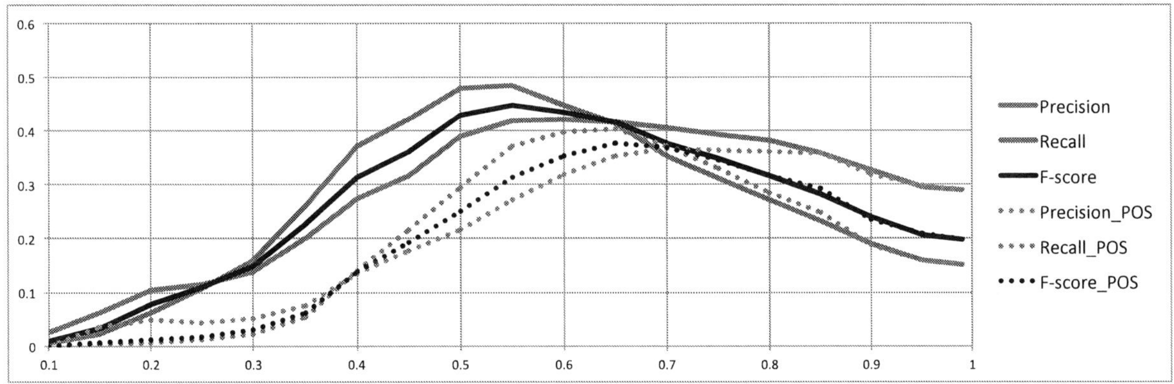

Figure 1: Results of Varseta strict matching with ANCHOR and the DLR similarity measure on raw (solid lines) and part-of-speech tagged data (dotted lines). Similarity level thresholds on x-axis; precision, recall and F-score on y-axis.

dard was 0.55 for DLR, and 0.51 for EDR (see Figure 1).

While performing experiments on the Swedish gold standard data, we found that the ANCHOR strategy with the DLR similarity measure performed slightly better relative to the gold standard annotation.

Additionally, we experimented on including information from the part-of-speech tagging of the transcripts in such away that the pair of strings compared consisted of both the words and their part-of-speech tags. Our intuition was that this might give a more refined analysis, for example, by distinguishing cases of homonymy. This version of the algorithm turned out not to improve performance, however (see Figure 1), and was therefore dropped.

5 Results: Automated extraction of variation sets

5.1 Evaluation against the Swedish gold standard

We evaluated the Varseta tool against the gold standard using two kinds of metrics, which we refer to as *strict* and *fuzzy* matching. Strict matching requires exact matching on the utterance level of the extracted variation set and the corresponding gold standard set, whereas fuzzy matching allows for partial overlaps of the extracted variation set and the gold standard set. In the example in Table 3, only utterance 3 and 4 are members of the gold standard variation set, whereas the algorithm extracts utterances 1–4. Hence, the strict matching metric treats

this extracted set as a false positive, whereas the fuzzy matching metric treats it as a true positive.

Table 4 summarizes the results of extraction of variation sets relative to the gold standard according to the strict and fuzzy metric. Strict F-score reaches 0.577 and fuzzy F-score reaches 0.813 for age group 1, but F-scores gradually decrease with increasing age.

This observed phenomenon has two reasons: first, the decrease in the proportion of exact repetitions as the child grows older; second, the increasing complexity of the parent's speech. As the complexity increases, capturing variation requires more than surface-based methods. This finding is in line with (Wirén et al., 2016).

5.2 Extraction of variation sets in 26 languages

For exploration of repetition and variation in child-directed speech in 26 languages, as captured in CHILDES-26-VS, we have used the Varseta tool.

We expected to find decreasing **proportions of utterances in variation sets** as a function of child age for all languages.

The findings for a majority of languages, 19 out of 26 (Irish, Welsh, Cantonese, Indonesian, Japanese, Afrikaans, Danish, Dutch, English, German, Swedish, Italian, Spanish, Croatian, Russian, Estonian, Farsi, Greek, and Turkish), indicate a decrease in the proportion of utterances in variation sets as a function of child age (see bold face proportions in table 5 on page 7).

We have observed exceptions in Chinese, Thai, Catalan, French, Portuguese, Hebrew, and Tamil.

Example utterances	Member of gold set	Extracted by algorithm
1. *Ska vi lägga ner nånting i i väskan då?* ('Are we going to put something in in the bag then?')	–	Yes
2. *Va?* ('Huh?')	–	Yes
3. *Ska du lägga ner kossan i väskan kanske?* ('Are you going to put down the cow in the bag maybe?')	Yes	Yes
4. *Ska vi lägga ner kossan?* ('Are we going to put down the cow?')	Yes	Yes

Table 3: Example variation set from the gold standard (utterance 3–4) and utterances extracted by the Varseta tool (utterance 1–4).

String matching relative to gold standard	Group 1 0;7–0;9	Group 2 1;0–1;2	Group 3 1;4–1;7	Group 4 2;3–2;9
ANCHOR				
Strict precision	0.554	0.415	0.337	0.164
Strict recall	0.603	0.460	0.473	0.282
Strict *F*-score	**0.577**	0.437	0.393	0.208
INCREMENTAL				
Strict precision	0.549	0.476	0.416	0.415
Strict recall	0.559	0.418	0.453	0.436
Strict *F*-score	0.554	**0.445**	**0.433**	**0.425**
ANCHOR				
Fuzzy precision	0.779	0.634	0.548	0.358
Fuzzy recall	0.849	0.703	0.770	0.615
Fuzzy *F*-score	**0.813**	**0.667**	**0.640**	0.453
INCREMENTAL				
Fuzzy precision	0.736	0.621	0.553	0.537
Fuzzy recall	0.748	0.545	0.601	0.564
Fuzzy *F*-score	0.742	0.581	0.576	**0.550**

Table 4: Evaluation of the Varseta tool for automatic variation-set extraction against the Swedish gold standard per age group.

For Chinese, Thai, Hebrew, and Tamil, there are insufficient amounts of data for earlier age groups (age groups 2, 1, 2, and 1, respectively) which skews the proportion in comparison to older age groups. For instance, Chinese age group 2 contains 294 utterances and Chinese age group 3 contains 1395. In the age groups with sufficient/comparable amounts of data for these three languages, we do observe the expected decrease pattern.

However, data insufficiency or incomparability cannot explain the unexpected findings for French and Portugese, and thus in-depth analysis of these transcripts is needed.

For most of the languages the similar pattern of decrease in **proportion of exact repetitions** cannot be observed. One general trend is that the proportion of exact repetitions is small as compared to the proportion of utterances in variation sets. Exceptions to this trend are observed in Swedish, Danish, English, Russian, Cantonese, Japanese, Thai, Welsh, Estonian, Hebrew, and Tamil (average proportion of exact repetition: 0.13 in age group 1, 0.096 in age group 2, 0.066 in age group 3, and 0.04 in age group 4).

For some languages we observe a decrease in proportions, even to no exact repetitions, for example in German, French, Italian, Spanish, Farsi, and Turkish. A close inspection of these data files revealed

Lang. group	Language		Age groups 1	2	3	4
Celtic	Irish	a	–	–	862	899
		b	–	–	**0.63**	**0.39**
		c	–	–	0.03	0.05
	Welsh	a	–	–	304	226
		b	–	–	**0.54**	**0.23**
		c	–	–	0.11	0.04
EastAsian	Cantonese	a	–	–	392	1278
		b	–	–	**0.65**	**0.58**
		c	–	–	0.07	0.04
	Chinese	a	–	294	1395	1338
		b	–	*0.57*	**0.64**	**0.57**
		c	–	0.02	0.04	0.02
	Indonesian	a	–	–	577	714
		b	–	–	**0.58**	**0.50**
		c	–	–	0.05	0.05
	Japanese	a	220	281	525	1315
		b	**0.91**	**0.79**	**0.62**	**0.60**
		c	0.17	0.10	0.04	0.06
	Thai	a	123	222	172	250
		b	*0.42*	*0.50*	*0.49*	*0.51*
		c	0.07	0.03	0.03	0.02
Germanic	Afrikaans	a	–	–	87	128
		b	–	–	**0.56**	**0.54**
		c	–	–	0.09	0.00
	Danish	a	136	630	250	582
		b	**0.82**	**0.65**	**0.67**	**0.53**
		c	0.23	0.13	0.10	0.05
	Dutch	a	–	–	989	1176
		b	–	–	**0.52**	**0.50**
		c	–	–	0.06	0.03
	English	a	–	–	926	391
		b	–	–	**0.54**	**0.44**
		c	–	–	0.08	0.07
	German	a	82	62	1160	586
		b	**0.77**	**0.55**	0.51	0.54
		c	0.07	0.00	0.04	0.10
	Swedish[10]	a	1032	1421	1483	724
		b	**0.61**	**0.43**	**0.52**	**0.36**
		c	0.18	0.08	0.07	0.04

Lang. group	Language		Age groups 1	2	3	4
Romance	Catalan	a	–	–	47	264
		b	–	–	*0.45*	*0.61*
		c	–	–	0.09	0.02
	French	a	420	281	450	308
		b	*0.38*	*0.49*	*0.41*	*0.49*
		c	0.00	0.05	0.04	0.06
	Italian	a	–	–	368	541
		b	–	–	**0.46**	**0.37**
		c	–	–	0.01	0.00
	Portuguese	a	–	–	783	660
		b	–	–	*0.57*	*0.61*
		c	–	–	0.04	0.01
	Spanish	a	81	44	122	221
		b	**0.70**	**0.57**	**0.45**	**0.25**
		c	0.05	0.00	0.00	0.00
Slavic	Croatian	a	39	217	408	–
		b	**0.85**	**0.54**	**0.50**	–
		c	0.00	0.09	0.05	–
	Russian	a	–	–	1088	545
		b	–	–	**0.35**	**0.24**
		c	–	–	0.06	0.05
Other	Estonian	a	58	527	420	383
		b	**0.62**	0.37	0.43	0.41
		c	0.10	0.03	0.02	0.02
	Farsi	a	–	–	103	32
		b	–	–	**0.64**	**0.41**
		c	–	–	0.00	0.00
	Greek	a	–	–	246	453
		b	–	–	**0.56**	**0.48**
		c	–	–	0.06	0.07
	Hebrew	a	–	132	156	108
		b	–	*0.51*	*0.68*	*0.65*
		c	–	0.08	0.08	0.04
	Tamil	a	54	239	220	182
		b	*0.65*	*0.82*	*0.68*	*0.70*
		c	0.04	0.08	0.07	0.04
	Turkish	a	–	–	567	322
		b	–	–	**0.50**	**0.46**
		c	–	–	0.01	0.01

Table 5: Results of the ANCHOR-DLR strategy for automatic variation-set extraction applied to CHILDES-26-VS. Results are grouped by CHILDES language group (col. 1) and language (col. 2). For each language, a) the number of utterances, b) the proportion of utterances in variation sets, and c) the proportion of exact repetitions per age groups 1 (0;6–0;11), 2 (1;0–1;3), 3 (1;4–1;11), and 4 (2;0–2;9). Proportions in bold face follow expectations, whereas proportions in italics do not.

that this is not only the effect of the absence of exact repetitions, but also due to the level of analysis added to the transcripts, for instance markup for perceived pause length or prosody, comments in English, etc.

We also note that about half of the transcripts in Cantonese, Chinese, and Japanese were in latin characters, whereas e.g., some of the transcripts in age group 2 are in Chinese characters. Transcripts written in such logographic systems have a more compressed representation on the utterance level, and thus the similarity measure might need an adjustment.

In addition to quantitative trends across the languages, Varseta also provides variation sets for inspection. Here are two examples of automatically extracted variation sets in German and Farsi.

> *wo sind die anderen flaschen?* ('where are the other bottles?')[11]
> *guck mal da unten bei dem auto.* ('look down there by the car.')
> *da is noch eine flasche.* ('there is one bottle.')
> *da sin die anderen flaschen.* ('there are the other bottles.')

> *ho gorbe chi mige?* ('what does the cat say?')[12]
> *gorbehe ci mige?* ('what does the cat say?')
> *chi mige?* ('what does it say?')
> *mamaoushe chi mige?* ('what does ?(the mouse's mother) say?')
> *mamoushe chi?* ('?(the mouse's mother) what?')

6 Discussion

The evaluation of the Varseta tool for Swedish indicates that variation sets are easier to capture for earlier age groups (ANCHOR fuzzy F-score: 0.813, 0.667, 0.640 and 0.453 for age groups 1, 2, 3 and 4). The F-score reflects on the complexity of the input,

that is, not only the proportion of exact repetitions, but also patterns of expansion, insertion, deletion, word order change, and lexical substitution over sequences of utterances. Further, the algorithm does not include information on speaker turns as this information is not available in the current version of the corpus, and it is likely that this contributes to the low precision in the later dyads. According to the definition we follow, child vocalizations are allowed within a variation set (c.f., Wirén et al., 2016), but when such a child utterance constitutes a legitimate turn, the variation set should be split in two. Overall, the performance is according to what can be expected from a simple surface-based method. To our knowledge this is the only extraction method that has been evaluated against a manually annotated gold standard and therefore can serve as a baseline method for similar investigations.

The Varseta tool offers both quantitative analysis of repetition and variation in speech transcripts, and output in the form of sequences of utterances from those transcripts that constitute variation sets.

With regards to the analysis of the CHILDES-26-VS with the Varseta tool, the expected decrease in proportion of utterances in variation sets was observed for the majority of languages. The same observation cannot be made for the proportion of exact repetitions. This may be due to differences in transcription, for example regarding utterance segmentation and pause markup, between corpora in CHILDES. For instance, the Varseta tool cannot recognize variation in this example, as within-utterance repetition is not recognized by the tool. The short intervals, here marked by '(.)', may in another corpus constitute segmentation boundaries:

> *canta lá (.) canta (.) tu sabes?* ('sing there (.) sing (.) you know?')[13]
> *canta com o patinho.* ('sing with the duckling.')

The current method does not take into account semantic variation, complete lexical substitution, and other forms of complex variation. The surface-based approach can be improved by adapting semantic similarity methods like Word2Vec (Mikolov et al.,

---

[11]Example from CHILDES German/Szagun/NH/Celina/cel10400.cha, PID: 11312/c-00024238-1.

[12]Example from CHILDES Other/Farsi/Samadi/Shahrzad/sha108.cha, PID: 11312/c-00026963-1. English translations are approximate.

[13]Example from CHILDES Romance/Portuguese/Santos/Ines/1-7-6.cha, @PID: 11312/c-00037400-1

2013) as a possible solution for capturing lexical substitutions.

7   Conclusion

This study expands the scope of previous work by using a large-scale cross-language approach to exploring repetition and variation in child-directed speech. Further, the approach proposed in this paper on extracting variation sets from transcripts of child-directed speech is language-independent and automatic. The Varseta tool uses two surface-based strategies for automatic variation set detection which were evaluated against a gold standard corpus MINGLE-3-VS. The software, the gold standard corpus of Swedish, and the comparable corpus of 26 languages derived from CHILDES are freely available for exploration of repetition and variation in child-directed speech.

We have also reported findings on repetition and variation in child-directed speech in 26 languages, as captured in CHILDES-26-VS, using the Varseta tool. We expected to find decreasing proportions of utterances in variation sets as a function of child age for all languages. The findings confirmed this expectation for a majority of languages, except for French and Portuguese.

Acknowledgments

This research is part of the project "Modelling the emergence of linguistic structures in early childhood", funded by the Swedish Research Council (project 2011-675-86010-31). The development of the Varseta package (inkl. data) has been supported by an infrastructure grant from the Swedish Research Council (SWE-CLARIN, project 821-2013-2003). Thanks to Lisa Tengstrand and Claudia Eklås Tejman for annotation work, and Annika Otsa for extracting and preparing the CHILDES data. Ghazaleh Vafaeian provided the Farsi translation. Finally, we would like to thank the three anonymous reviewers for valuable comments.

References

Kristina Nilsson Björkenstam, Mats Wirén, and Robert Östling. 2016. Modelling the informativeness and timing of non-verbal cues in parent–child interaction. In *Proceedings of the 7th Workshop on Cognitive Aspects of Computational Language Learning, August 11, 2016, Association for Computational Linguistics*, pages 82–90, Berlin, Germany.

Paul E. Black. 2004. Ratcliff/Obershelp pattern recognition. *Dictionary of Algorithms and Data Structures*, 17.

Peter Brodsky, Heidi R. Waterfall, and Shimon Edelman. 2007. Characterizing motherese: On the computational structure of child-directed language. In *Proc. 29th Cognitive Science Society Conference*, Nashville, TN.

Erika Hoff-Ginsberg. 1986. Function and structure in maternal speech: Their relation to the child's development of syntax. *Developmental Psychology*, 22(3):155–163.

Erika Hoff-Ginsberg. 1990. Maternal speech and the child's development of syntax: a further look. *Journal of Child Language*, 17:85–99.

Nini Hoiting and Dan I. Slobin. 2002. What a deaf child needs to see: Advantages of a natural sign language over a sign system. In R. Schulmeister and H. Reinitzer, editors, *Progress in sign language research. In honor of Siegmund Prillwitz/Fortschritte in der Gebärdensprachforschung. Festschrift für Siegmund Prillwitz*, pages 268–277. Signum, Hamburg.

Aylin C. Küntay and Dan I. Slobin. 1996. Listening to a turkish mother: Some puzzles for acquisition. In *Social Interaction, Social Context, and Language. Essays in the Honor of Susan Ervin-Tripp*, pages 265–286. Lawrence Erlbaum, Mahwah, NJ.

Aylin C. Küntay and Dan I. Slobin. 2002. Putting interaction back into child language: Examples from Turkish. *Psychology of Language and Communication*, 6:5–14.

Francisco Lacerda. 2009. On the emergence of early linguistic functions: A biological and interactional perspective. In M. Lindgren M. Roll K. Alter, M. Horne and J. von Koss Torkildsen, editors, *Brain Talk: Discourse with and in the brain*, pages 207–230. Media-Tryck, Lund, Sweden.

Vladimir I. Levenshtein. 1966. Binary codes capable of correcting deletions, insertions, and reversals. In *Soviet physics doklady*, volume 10, pages 707–710.

Brian MacWhinney. 2000. *The CHILDES Project: Tools for analyzing talk*. Lawrence Erlbaum Associates, Mahwah, NJ, 3 edition.

Tomas Mikolov, Kai Chen, Greg Corrado, and Jeffrey Dean. 2013. Efficient estimation of word representations in vector space. *CoRR*, abs/1301.3781.

Anat Ninio, Catherine E. Snow, Barbara A. Pan, and Pamela R. Rollins. 1994. Classifying communicative acts in children's interactions. *Journal of Communicative Disorders*, 27:157–187.

Luca Onnis, Heidi R. Waterfall, and Shimon Edelman. 2008. Learn locally, act globally: Learning language from variation set cues. *Cognition*, 109(3):423–430.

Robert Östling. 2013. Stagger: an open-source part of speech tagger for Swedish. *Northern European Journal of Language Technology*, 3:1–18.

Heidi R. Waterfall, Ben Sandbank, Luca Onnis, and Shimon Edelman. 2010. An empirical generative framework for computational modeling of language acquisition. *Journal of Child Language*, 37:671–703.

Heidi R. Waterfall. 2006. *A Little Change is a Good Thing: Feature Theory, Language Acquisition and Variation Sets*. Ph.D. thesis, Department of Linguistics, University of Chicago.

Mats Wirén, Kristina Nilsson Björkenstam, Gintare Grigonyte, and Elisabet Eir Cortes. 2016. Longitudinal studies of variation sets in child-directed speech. In *Proceedings of the 7th Workshop on Cognitive Aspects of Computational Language Learning, August 11, 2016, Association for Computational Linguistics*, pages 44–52, Berlin, Germany.

P. Wittenburg, H. Brugman, A. Russel, A. Klassmann, and H. Sloetjes. 2006. ELAN: a professional framework for multimodality research. In *Proceedings of LREC 2006, Fifth International Conference on Language Resources and Evaluation*, pages 1556–1559, Genoa, Italy, May. ELRA.

Validating Bundled Gap Filling – Empirical Evidence for Ambiguity Reduction and Language Proficiency Testing Capabilities

Niklas Meyer
Language Technology Lab
University of Duisburg Essen
Duisburg, Germany

Michael Wojatzki
Language Technology Lab
University of Duisburg Essen
Duisburg, Germany

Torsten Zesch
Language Technology Lab
University of Duisburg Essen
Duisburg, Germany

Abstract

Bundled gap filling exercises (Wojatzki et al., 2016) were recently introduced as a promising new exercise type to complement or even replace single gap-fill tasks. However, it is not yet confirmed that the applied creation method works properly and it is still to be investigated if bundled gap-fill tests are a suitable method for assessing language proficiency. In this paper, we address both issues by varying the construction methods and by conducting a user study with 75 participants in which we also measure externally validated language proficiency. We find that the originally proposed way to construct bundles is indeed minimizing their ambiguity, but that further investigation is needed to determine which aspects of language proficiency they are actually measuring.

1 Introduction

Gap filling tasks, also known as cloze tests (Taylor, 1953), are a frequently used for language learning and proficiency testing. The test taker is asked to restore a word that has been omitted from a text or sentence. However, people involved in designing and scoring gap-fill tests are frequently confronted with two major problems: ambiguity and lack of automatability. Ambiguity means that in traditional gap-fill tests frequently more than one word can be used for a gap (Chavez-Oller et al., 1985). For example, the gap in *The kids have to ___ their own lunch* could be filled with *make*, *bring*, *prepare*, or *eat*. However, this fact is often not taken into consideration when it comes to scoring and only one solution is scored as correct. This can lead to high error rates, even with native speakers (Klein-Braley and Raatz, 1982).

Alternatively, there are approaches which allow a set of acceptable solutions, which can improve the validity of gap-fill tests in terms of higher correlations to other tests that measure language proficiency (Brown, 1980). However, this comes at the cost of a higher manual workload and higher subjectivity. An extension of this idea is to weigh the words according to their occurrence in the solutions of participants (Darnell, 1968). However, it could be shown that this scoring procedure has a negative impact on the validity (Brown, 1980).

A way to address these problems is the use of multiple answers, usually the correct solution along with three distractors. The distractors can, however, heavily influence the difficulty of the task. Additionally, using distractors changes the nature of the task from producing a solution to recognizing a solution (Wesche and Paribakht, 1994).

Wojatzki et al. (2016) have recently introduced *bundled gap filling* as an alternative form of gap-filling exercises with a set of gaps in several different sentences, all hiding the same single word. In such an exercise, the learner is confronted with all of the gaps in a bundle at the same time and asked to find the single word to restore all of them correctly. Figure 1 shows examples for all three types of exercises. Wojatzki et al. (2016) showed that the generated bundles decrease ambiguity, but it is still unclear whether the ambiguity reduction was due to their selection procedure or whether any selection of bundled sentences would achieve the same result. Another issue is that in the user study by Wojatzki et al. (2016) all participants had a very high language proficiency level which leaves the question how well bundles work for less proficient learners.

To further investigate these issues, we conducted a user study aimed at comparing the effectiveness

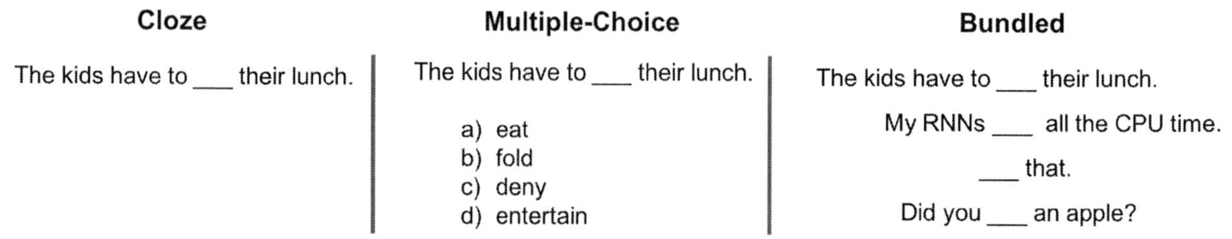

Cloze

The kids have to ___ their lunch.

Multiple-Choice

The kids have to ___ their lunch.

a) eat
b) fold
c) deny
d) entertain

Bundled

The kids have to ___ their lunch.

My RNNs ___ all the CPU time.

___ that.

Did you ___ an apple?

Figure 1: Comparison of exercise types.

of different strategies for computing bundles. In addition, we investigated the relationship between the proficiency level of the test takers and ability to correctly solve bundled gaps. We find that the bundle creation algorithm used by Wojatzki et al. (2016) is disambiguating bundles with a much higher accuracy compared to selecting sentences by chance, while under both conditions the difference to maximally ambiguous bundles is quite high. We also find that the ability to solve bundled gap-fill tasks is indeed substantially correlated ($r = .48$) with the language proficiency of the test takers as measured by *cTest* scores (Klein-Braley and Raatz, 1982). However, the far from perfect correlation implies that further investigation is needed in order to clarify which aspects of language proficiency is measured by bundled gap-fill tests.

2   Bundled Gap-Fill Exercises

In this section, we describe the principle behind bundled gap-fill exercises in order to locate the part of the algorithm that we wish to further validate.

The construction starts with selecting a target word with the surrounding context, i.e. usually a sentence. Depending on the type of exercise or test to be generated the sentence can be taken from a reading assignment, can be provided by a teacher, or can also be a random sentence containing the target word. The algorithm then iteratively adds more sentences to the bundle that contain the same target word. In each iteration the one sentence is selected that maximizes the probability of the target as gap filler for the whole bundle. For the purpose of validating this selection, we propose to select sentences at random and sentences that minimize the probability as competing strategies. We closely replicate the setup by Wojatzki et al. (2016) in our study in order to maximize comparability with their results.

Probability of Gap Fillers   We compute the probability of a word fitting the gap using an n-gram language model trained over the two billion word *ukWaC English Web Corpus* (Baroni et al., 2009). We utilize FASTSUBS (Yuret, 2012) with *additive smoothing* (Chen and Goodman, 1999) for efficiently computing the probabilities.

Sentence Base & Target Words   We use the GUM corpus (Zeldes, 2016) to select bundle sentences, and we also rely on the same target words as in the original study: four adjectives (*new, best, full, final*), four nouns (*people, language, information, room*), and four verbs (*make, want, add, give*).

Bundle Construction   In order to define a target function for unambiguous bundles, Wojatzki et al. (2016) defined the disambiguation level $D(b)$ of a gap bundle b as the log of the ratio between the probability of the target word t and the probability of the most likely word w other than t:

$$D(b) = log \frac{P(F(b) = t)}{\max_{w \in V \setminus \{t\}} P(F(b) = w)}$$

The greater this ratio, the more probable is the target word compared to any other word, and the gap bundle can thus be considered less ambiguous. This mechanism is exemplified in Figure 2.

Given this setup, a bundle for a certain sentence containing the target word is constructed by finding another sentence that contains the target word and which maximizes $D(b)$ for the whole bundle:

$$g_{i+1} = \arg \max_{g \in G_t \setminus b_i} (D(b_i \cup g)), \qquad (1)$$

where G is the sentence base and G_t is the set of gaps in G hiding the target word t.

We call this original strategy MAXIMIZE as it maximizes the disambiguation metric $D(b)$. Only

52

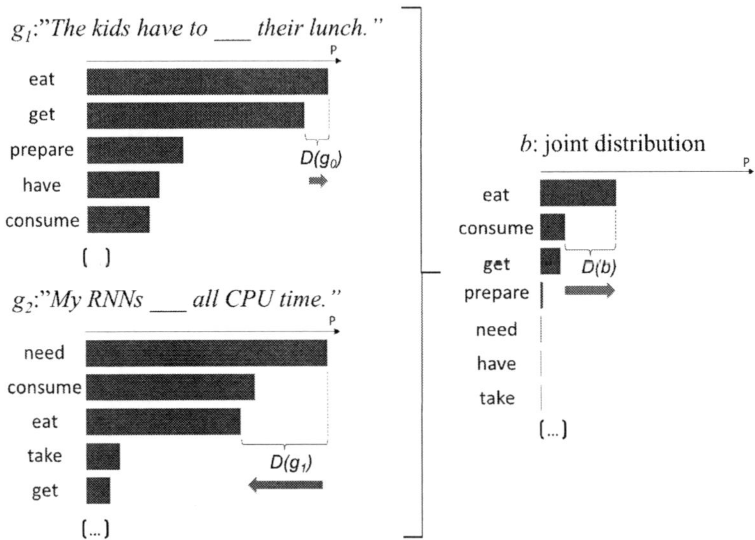

Figure 2: Two cloze tests for the target word *eat* are combined into a bundled cloze test. The diagram illustrates log probability of the possible solutions and how the disambiguation measure $D(b)$ is improved when calculated over the joint distribution.

testing this strategy might hide the fact that randomly selecting sentences with the target word are also likely to increase the disambiguation level. Therefore, we introduce a RANDOM configuration, in which we randomly select sentences. To get better insights into the range of values that the disambiguation level can fall into, we introduce another configuration called MINIMIZE where we change $\arg\max$ to $\arg\min$ in equation 1.

3 Experimental Setup

Given this setup, we can formulate the following research hypotheses:

1. RANDOM Using randomly created bundles results in more ambiguous bundles compared with the original MAXIMIZE setup.

2. MINIMIZE Using bundles that minimize $D(b)$ will lead to even more ambiguous bundles.

Additionally, we are interested in the influence of the language proficiency level of test takers on the success rate in the bundles. We assume that there will be an effect that shows that higher scores are obtained by people with greater proficiency in the English language. We hope to show that the scores in bundled gap-fill tests correlate highly with scores in other language tests, such as the *cTest*. We can thus formulate a third hypothesis:

3. PROFICIENCY There is a high correlation between a test taker's language proficiency and the score obtained when solving gap bundles.

3.1 User Study

To test our hypotheses, we conducted a user study. The study was taken by 118 people of which 75 fully completed the study (52 female, 1 not specified/other gender). As we have three conditions (MAXIMIZE, MINIMIZE, RANDOM, there are 25 participants per condition. The average age of the participants was 22.8 ($SD = 6.9$, ranging from 19 to 67 years). Most of the participants were university students currently enrolled at University of Duisburg-Essen. Additionally, the language proficiency of the participants was measured using a *cTest* that had to be solved after the bundles. For that purpose, we used a *cTest* constructed by the language teaching department of our university.

Participants were shown bundles with an increasing number of sentences. They first saw one sentence with the target word to be restored, then a second, then a third, then a fourth. After each sentence, they were asked to type in the word that (best) suits the gap(s).

Since the GUM corpus is a comparatively small corpus, there are few sentences containing rare words and thus few possible combinations of these sentences. Hence, from the 12 target words used by Wojatzki et al. (2016), we excluded *room* and *give*, as the bundles in all three experimental conditions were almost identical. Note that in future experiments, this problem could be solved by using a larger corpus from which the bundle sentences are selected.

4   Results & Discussion

In the following, we report and discuss the results of our study.

4.1   Bundle Construction

We first compare the different conditions for creating bundles that are tested in our study: MAXIMIZE, RANDOM, and MINIMIZE. For each condition, we measure the success rate after showing 1, 2, 3, or 4 bundle sentences. A detailed overview of the results per bundle is given in Figure 3, while Figure 4 shows the aggregated results.

As the first sentence is the same under all three conditions, we expect the success rate to be almost the same. The achieved results are close enough to argue that the three subgroups of participants are comparable. For larger bundle sizes, we observe that MAXIMIZE works best, MINIMIZE establishes a lower-bound, and RANDOM is somewhere in between. This shows that the utilized disambiguation measure is able to lower or increase the ambiguity of a bundle (although we usually only want to lower it). How well the RANDOM strategy is going to work largely depends on the properties of the underlying sentence base. If it contains a lot of similar contexts, the success rate might be much closer to the MINIMIZE condition.

Because MAXIMIZE is the same strategy for constructing bundles as was used by Wojatzki et al. (2016), we can compare our results with theirs. However, in their study, all participants had a very high proficiency level while this study was open to participants with different English levels. This explains why our success rates are in general a bit lower, but with the same trend of rising success rates from 1 to 4 sentences in the bundle. In our study the average success rate increases from .10 after only seeing the first sentence to .52 after the fourth. This is a close replication of the numbers from the original study where the increase was from .27 to .78.

Statistical Significance   In order to test whether these differences are real differences and not statistical noise, we statistically test our hypotheses. We look at the overall success rates per participant after seeing all four sentences, and conduct a one-way analysis of variance (ANOVA), which indeed confirms both, the MAXIMIZE and the RANDOM hypothesis ($F(2, 72) = 8.93$, $p < .001$). The differences after seeing only one sentence are not statistically significant ($p = .251$). In order to determine which conditions have significantly different arithmetic means, the two a-posteriori tests Scheffé (1953) and Tukey-HSD (Tukey, 1949) were used.[1] Both tests were significant for both combinations (MAXIMIZE, MINIMIZE: Tukey-HSD and Scheffé $p < .001$) and (MAXIMIZE, RANDOM: Tukey-HSD $p = .027$, Scheffé $p = .036$), which further confirms both research hypotheses.

4.2   Language Proficiency

As we have measured the language proficiency of participants using a *cTest*, we can correlate the *cTest* score with the bundle score (of the MAXMIZE condition) to examine whether bundled gap-fill exercises actually measure language proficiency. Figure 5 shows the corresponding scatterplot. The resulting Pearson correlation is $r = .48$. This shows that bundled gap-fill exercises can be used to measure language proficiency, but that both tests seem to measure slightly different constructs. Further research is needed to find out which aspects of language proficiency are actually measured by bundled gap filling exercises, and how bundles relate to other established testing methods.

5   Future Work

Since bundled gap filling is a very recent paradigm, there are various possibilities to deepen the understanding and the validation of the approach. In general, we see three major strands of future research: (i) an refinement of the approach itself, (ii) determining more influencing factors, and (iii) broadening the empirical evidence.

---

[1]An ANOVA can only implicate that there are generally differences, but is unable to determine which versions show significant differences. Scheffé and Tukey-HSD are the most frequently used post-hoc tests with Scheffé being considered very conservative in contrast to Tukey-HSD.

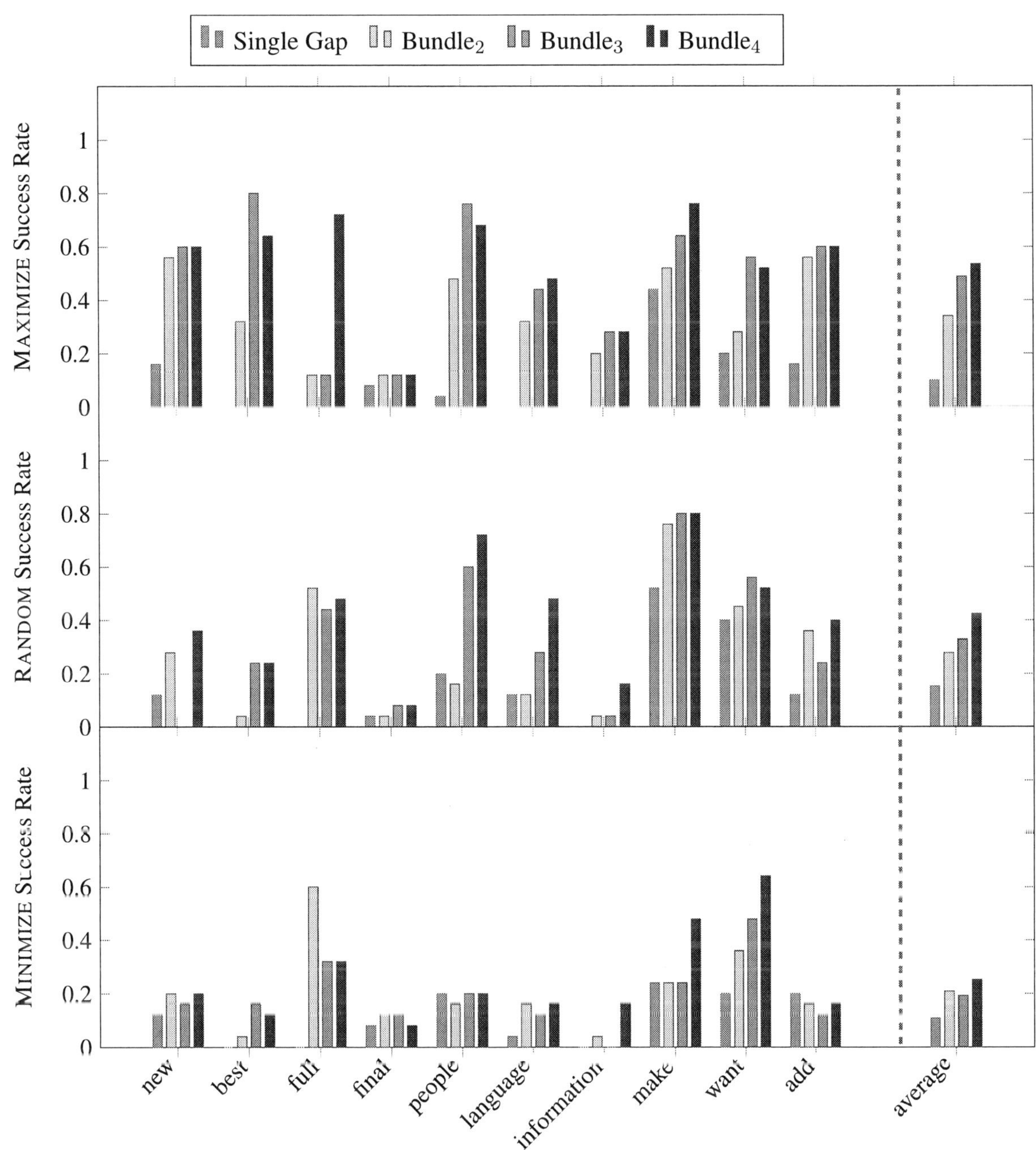

Figure 3: Success rate per item

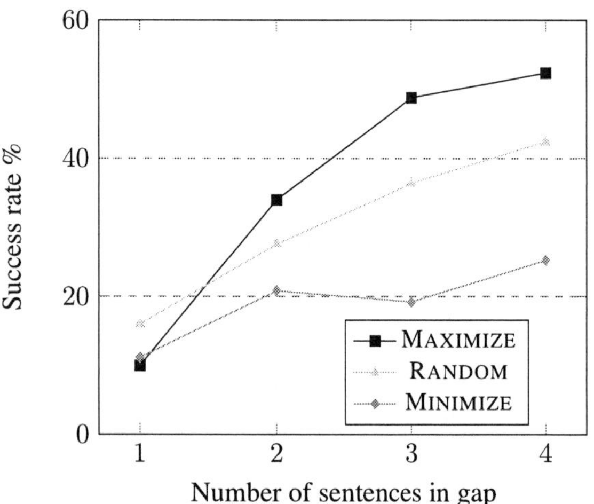

Figure 4: Comparison of strategies for creating bundles

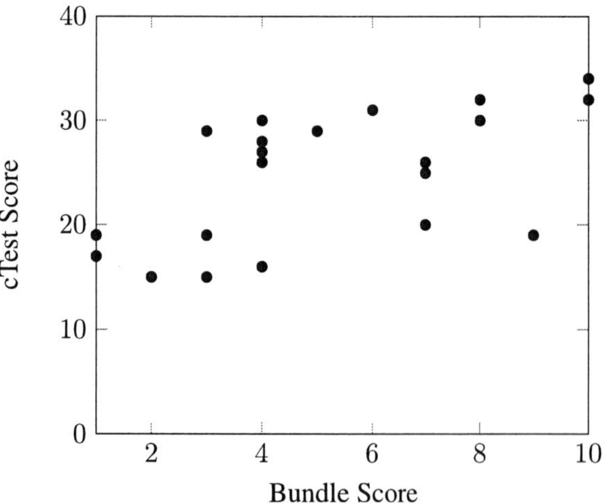

Figure 5: Influence of language proficiency on bundle scores

Refinement The approach for creating bundles could be improved along different lines. First, a different, larger corpus should be used which we expect to lead to even better bundles. Recall, that in the present study, we had to omit two target words which could have been avoided by using a larger corpus. Second, the probabilities of gap fillers have been estimated with a count-based language model. By nature, the used 5-gram model cannot incorporate a context bigger than four words around the gap. However, longer dependencies may indeed play a role when solving gap-fill tests (Bachman, 1982; Chihara et al., 1977). Consequently, future research should clarify whether more advanced language models which are capable of modeling long range dependencies result in even better bundles.

Influencing Factors A number of properties were found to influence the difficulty of gap-fill tests. As bundled gap filling is based on regular gap-fill tests, in future work it should be clarified whether the identified factors also affect the bundled version. The following properties have been shown to have an effect on the difficulty of gaps: Brown (1989) shows that the position of the gap in the sentence and the readability of the passage have an influence on the difficulty of the exercise. Characteristics of the omitted word that affect the difficulty are the length of the word (Abraham and Chapelle, 1992), whether the word is a function word or a content word (Kobayashi, 2002), the frequency of the word in the language (Kobayashi, 2002), and the word origin (Brown, 1989). Consequently, in future work, the set of target words should be systematically varied with respect to the mentioned factors.

Broadening Empirical Evidence In order to strengthen the empirical evidence, future work should aim at creating larger data sets which are closer to existing language learning or testing scenarios. For example, it should be investigated how bundles relate to other state-of-the-art language proficiency tests. For this purpose, bundles need to be introduced to a broader audience and to be integrated into official testing methods. This can help to generate an extensive amount of new data that can further verify bundled gap-filling and show their usefulness in real life scenarios compared to other testing methods. Furthermore, it would be interesting to see how well results could be reproduced for languages other than English.

The presented results may be biased by the small sample size of this study. Therefore, to further investigate bundled gap-filling and its differences to the *cTest*, it seems necessary to increase the number of test takers.

Last but not least, bundles are also a promising tool for language learning. However, before bringing bundled gap-filling to the classroom, the underlying implementation needs to be taken from prototype to production status. We are currently working on an improved version that we plan to make publicly available.

6   Conclusion

In this work, we have presented an empirical evaluation of *bundled gap filling* (Wojatzki et al., 2016). We confirm that the paradigm is capable of significantly reducing ambiguity in gap-fill exercises – a major problem of this popular exercise type. Moreover, we provide evidence that the originally proposed algorithm for creating bundles is well functioning. As bundled gap-fill scores only moderately correlate with the language proficiency of the participants as measured by a *cTest*, further research is required to determine the properties of bundles.

Acknowledgments

This work was partially supported by the Deutsche Forschungsgemeinschaft (DFG) under grant No. GRK 2167, Research Training Group "User-Centred Social Media". We thank the reviewers for their valuable and encouraging feedback.

References

Roberta G. Abraham and Carol A. Chapelle. 1992. The meaning of cloze test scores: An item difficulty perspective. *The Modern Language Journal*, 76(4):468–479.

Lyle F Bachman. 1982. The trait structure of cloze test scores. *Tesol Quarterly*, pages 61–70.

Marco Baroni, Silvia Bernardini, Adriano Ferraresi, and Eros Zanchetta. 2009. The {WaCky} wide web: a collection of very large linguistically processed web-crawled corpora. *Language Resources and Evaluation*, 43(3):209–226.

James Dean Brown. 1980. Relative merits of four methods for scoring cloze tests. *The Modern Language Journal*, 64(3):311–317.

James D. Brown. 1989. Cloze Item Difficulty. *JALT Journal*, 11(1):46–67.

Mary Anne Chavez-Oller, Tetsuro Chihara, Kelley A. Weaver, and John W. Oller. 1985. When are cloze items sensitive to constraints across sentences? *Language Learning*, 35(2):181–206.

Stanley F. Chen and Joshua Goodman. 1999. An Empirical Study of Smoothing Techniques for Language Modeling. *Computer Speech & Language*, 13(4):359–393.

Tetsuro Chihara, John Oller, Kelley Weaver, and Mary Anne Chavez-Oller. 1977. Are cloze items sensitive to constraints across sentences? *Language learning*, 27(1):63–70.

Donald K Darnell. 1968. The development of an english language proficiency test of foreign students, using a clozentropy procedure. final report.

Christine Klein-Braley and Ulrich Raatz. 1982. Der C-Test: ein neuer Ansatz zur Messung allgemeiner Sprachbeherrschung. *AKS-Rundbrief*, 4:23–37.

Miyoko Kobayashi. 2002. Cloze tests revisited: Exploring item characteristics with special attention to scoring methods. *The Modern Language Journal*, 86(4):571–586.

Henry Scheffé. 1953. A method for judging all contrasts in the analysis of variance. *Biometrika*, 40(1-2):87–110.

Wilson L. Taylor. 1953. "Cloze Procedure": A New Tool For Measuring Readability. *Journalism Quarterly*, 30(4):415–433.

John W Tukey. 1949. Comparing individual means in the analysis of variance. *Biometrics*, pages 99–114.

Marjorie Wesche and Sima T. Paribakht. 1994. Enhancing Vocabulary Acquisition through Reading: A Hierarchy of Text-Related Exercise Types. Paper presented at the AAAL '94 Conference.

Michael Wojatzki, Oren Melamud, and Torsten Zesch. 2016. Bundled gap filling: A new paradigm for unambiguous cloze exercises. In *Proceedings of the 11th Workshop on Innovative Use of NLP for Building Educational Applications*, pages 172–181, San Diego, CA, June. Association for Computational Linguistics.

Deniz Yuret. 2012. FASTSUBS: An efficient and exact procedure for finding the most likely lexical substitutes based on an n-gram language model. *Signal Processing Letters, IEEE*, 19(11):725–728.

Amir Zeldes. 2016. The GUM Corpus: Creating Multilayer Resources in the Classroom. *Language Resources and Evaluation*, pages 1–32.

Appendix

These are the bundles that were used in the study for the MAXIMIZE condition. All conditions had the same first sentences. Participants were first confronted with only the first sentence, then the second, third and finally the fourth. In total, there were ten bundles.

add

1. Try not to make your words sound like utter and complete gibberish just ____________ a little extra than our regular English language.

2. Put the cider vinegar into a small bowl and ____________ the soy milk .

3. ____________ the wet ingredients to the dry ingredients and beat together (by hand or with an electric hand-held mixer).

4. Here 's a great vegan cupcake recipe to use as a base for whatever flavored icing you want to ____________to it.

best

1. They followed ____________ practices for anatomical preservation.

2. Just east of Broadway and continuing north and south is Oakland's famous Chinatown, and that to get the real essence of "Chinatown," Oakland rather than San Francisco is your ____________ bet.

3. To this day, about 10 or 12 of these World War II Japanese shipwrecks comprise what is considered one of the ____________ dive sites in the world.

4. Here 's a great vegan cupcake recipe to use as a base for whatever flavored icing you want to ____________to it.

final

1. Not all were pleased with the ____________ choice of locations.

2. A ____________ thought.

3. The stampede at Islam's most holy site happened at Jamarat Bridge, during an event where pebbles are thrown at a pillar to represent the stoning of Satan as part of the ____________ rites of the Hajj.

4. Many people choose to leave out the green, which is lime if you're using original Skittles, and purple, which is grape in the original style, as they can create a weird taste combination or a less than appealing color for the ____________ product.

information

1. First, people around the world are desperate for high quality how-to ____________.

2. The city maintains several tourist offices, all of which can offer helpful ____________ on accommodation, free maps, and bus connections.

3. I don't have enough ____________ to answer this question, one way or the other.

4. The Visitors' Center provides ____________ on the role of Fort Lee in the War.

language

1. Make sure that it is a ____________ that while speaking, you don't get a literal knot in your tongue!

2. As they design their web pages for the newer browsers with advanced web technology and geared to the newest web core markup ____________ HTML 5, they are forced to accommodate older out-of-date technology to support IE6 users.

3. Be fluent in your own made up ____________ and start spreading this to your friends, family and strangers!

4. Write your own poem/novel/story with your own made up ____________.

make

1. However, paying people to write and edit articles ultimately means that you have to ___________ one of two sacrifices.

2. In the 1960s and 1970s, many 19th century neoclassical buildings, often small and private, were demolished to ___________ way for office buildings, often designed by great Greek architects.

3. The single most costly thing we spend on is rent and advertising, those two together ___________ up the bulk of what we spend.

4. You should ___________ sure that your clothing covers at least your shoulders and your knees and some places may require that you wear ankle-length pants or skirts and long sleeved tops.

new

1. We took quite a few ___________ girls over there back then in 2005, leading into the World Cup in the Netherlands.

2. Athens today is ever evolving, forging a brand ___________ identity for the 21st century.

3. The Museum of Flight in Seattle, Washington was also proposed as another location for a shuttle, going so far as to build a ___________ building to house an orbiter.

4. In March, a bundle of blueprints for a ___________ headquarters for the military's counterterrorism unit were found stuffed in the trash on a downtown street.

people

1. It emphasizes consumerism, the belief that success always goes to ___________ who merit it due to their abilities, dedication and qualifications, and reinforces, rather than changes, existing ideas related to gender, ethnicity and nationality.

2. On the other hand, this isn't to say that you should necessarily make jokes at other ___________'s expense, as this can make you seem mean and petty.

3. Telling good jokes is an art that comes naturally to some ___________, but for others it takes practice and hard work.

4. Moreover, electing a third-party governor represents a repudiation of politics as usual, and the major party legislators will face changed constraints and incentives, meaning that much more is possible than many ___________ assume, especially with strong leadership.

want

1. Why did she so badly ___________ to attend?

2. For instance, you might say something like: "If you like those guys, you might ___________ to check out this band called Manic Albatross - they're like the Beatles, only darker.

3. How do you approach the difficult challenge of talking to the Palestinians when, in the end, they dont ___________ Israel to exist.

4. "We ___________ to thank all of the locations that expressed an interest in one of these national treasures," said Bolden to the gathered crowd which contained many KSC employees.

full

1. However, the ___________ fuselage trainer, that every astronaut including [former Museum of Flight CEO] Bonnie Dunbar has been trained on, will soon call the Museum of Flight home.

2. Another thing non-locals don't often realize is that Cleveland's long history of industrial wealth has left it chock ___________ of cultural riches as well as the beginnings of a "sustainable city" movement.

3. If you buy too many boxes you can return the unused for a ___________ refund.

4. York is ___________ of magic and a wonderful place to bring children!

Faking Intelligent CALL: the Irish context and the road ahead

Neasa Ní Chiaráin and **Ailbhe Ní Chasaide**
The Phonetics and Speech Lab.
Centre for Language and Communication Studies
Trinity College, Dublin
neasa.nichiarain@tcd.ie

Abstract

Speech-enabled dialogue systems developed within an iCALL framework offer a potentially powerful tool for dealing with the challenges of teaching/learning an endangered language where learners have limited access to native speaker models of the language and limited exposure to the language in a truly communicative setting. This paper explores the major potential of virtual conversational agent systems with inbuilt simulated 'intelligence' for the Irish (endangered) language context.

1   Introduction

Multimodal dialogue systems with inbuilt simulated 'intelligence' have huge potential in language learning/teaching environments. In the context of the many minority/endangered languages, such as Irish (Gaelic), these systems could make even more of an impact. Major difficulties exist for language learners related to the lack of exposure to native speaker models and creating virtual 'native speakers' to converse with learners opens new paths towards overcoming these issues in the socio-linguistic context of endangered languages. Many languages, and particularly minority, endangered and under-resourced languages lack several of the linguistic and technological prerequisites for the construction of 'intelligent' dialogue partners. Nonetheless, as will be illustrated here, interim solutions are possible, which can offer partial dialogue systems, which can still have impact in the teaching/learning context.

Following a brief discussion of the socio-linguistic context of current developments for Irish, this paper presents (i) a simulated intelligent dialogue partner, constructed for Irish language tuition, using synthetic voices and an animated avatar (a talking monkey), (ii) a discussion on how, in the absence of NLP-based resources (yet to be developed for Irish), specific strategies are adopted which allow the impression of 'intelligent' discourse with an agent, and (iii) an outline of the steps envisaged to allow a fuller, more 'intelligent' system, using NLP resources.

2   The socio-linguistic context of Irish language teaching/learning

Irish is the first official language of the Republic of Ireland and is a working language of the European Union. Yet, it is an endangered language (Moseley, 2010) in that it has no monolingual speakers and there are few, if any, domains where Irish is the sole acceptable language. Irish is a compulsory subject of study for all pupils attending second level schools in the Republic of Ireland. Teachers, however, are often second language learners and therefore there is huge variation in levels of proficiency ranging from relatively low communicative competence to traditional native speakers. At second level the recommended annual taught time for Irish is 110 contact hours per year (Eurydice, 2013, p. 10) which means learners lack sufficient input: far more exposure to the language than what is currently available within school hours is needed. The use of interactive language learning technology in schools is extremely limited and the use of antiquated and dull teaching materials (and sometimes methods) adds further to low levels of motivation.

Since motivation is generally accepted as being the prime factor associated with successful language learning (Robichaud, 2014), the development of virtual world platforms where the learner can interact with an artificial interlocutor/dialogue partner and create the semblance of a natural conversation seems appropriate. The learner can become engaged with the target language and use it to complete specific tasks or engage in games. Though the development of such platforms is still in its infancy, the concept would seem to have a particular attraction in the case of minority or endangered languages.

3   A provisional interim dialogue partner

In the major world languages much effort has been put into creating speech activities which allow learners to engage in spoken interaction with a conversational partner, the most difficult competence for a learner to acquire independently. An initial attempt at providing opportunity for students of Irish to practice conversation is presented here as *Taidhgín*, (pronounced: [tˠ aɪ ɟ iː nʲ]), an 'intelligent' dialogue partner in the form of an animated, smartly dressed monkey. *Taidhgín* was built using Artificial Intelligence Markup Language (AIML), an XML-based open-source programming language which was developed by Richard Wallace and the Alicebot free software community during the period 1995-2000. *Taidhgín* is hosted and run from Pandorabots which is a 'free open-source-based community web service which enables you to develop and publish chatbots on the web' (pandorabots.com). *Taidhgín* has integrated Irish language synthetic voices which are developed as part of the ABAIR initiative (www.abair.ie) in Trinity College, Dublin. Ideally, the chatbot presented here would form part of an end-to-end spoken dialogue system with speech input and output but as there is not yet an automatic speech recognition system for the Irish language, the user must input speech to the *Taidhgín* system by typing into a text box.

Figure 1: *Taidhgín:* the prototype dialogue partner.

Evaluations of *Taidhgín* were carried out nationwide in 13 schools by 228 pupils. The evaluations consisted of (1) eliciting learners' opinions of the overall chatbot platform as a learning environment and (2) evaluating the intelligibility, quality, and attractiveness of the ABAIR text-to-speech synthetic voices used in this platform. Results were very positive to both the learning platform and to the synthetic voices, evidenced by an evaluation by 228 16-17 year old learners of Irish, 73% of whom rated 'intelligibility' at points 4 or 5 (positive or very positive) on a Likert scale; 73% rated same for 'quality'; and 53% rated same for 'attractiveness'. This demonstrates that even a partially 'intelligent' system which exploits speech and language technologies stands to have immediate impact in the Irish educational context. For a fuller account of evaluations see Ní Chiaráin & Ní Chasaide (2016). Further evaluations were carried out on proficient speakers of Irish who are teachers and results were also found to yield similarly high ratings (Ní Chiaráin, 2014).

The Pandorabots system presented here is based on pattern matching whereby all likely responses to *Taidhgín*'s questions are hardcoded. Therefore much content development work was needed in order to give a certain appearance of intelligence to *Taidhgín*, as the system began with no initial Irish language content. The most common errors (grammatical and orthographic) made by Irish Leaving Certificate students (pre-University examinations) have been documented in work by Ó Baoill (1981) and this information was used in the development of *Taidhgín* to build an internal correction system. Currently the most commonly made errors are hardcoded into the system: when learner input is matched to these errors *Taidhgín*

Version used by *Taidhgín* chatbot	Translation
Human: Tá **dhá** dearth[á]ir agam. ***Taidhgín*:** Ó, tuigim – **beirt** deartháir! Níl aon deirfiúr agat, buachaillí ar fad atá sa teach leat! Agus, an bhfuil na deartháireacha seo níos óige nó níos sine ná tusa?	***Human: I have *two brothers.*** ***Taidhgín: Oh, I understand – two brothers! You've no sister, all boys in the house! And are these brothers younger or older than you?***

Figure 2: *Taidhgín* feedback: reformulating learner input and recasting the corrected version

reprises a correct version as part of his response. This manner of correction avoids a break in the flow of conversation, which explicit correction would entail. An example of this is presented in Figure 2 and discussed further below.

In addition to this recasting correction mechanism, the log files are made available to the learner and tutor for later review. The grammar and spelling checkers which are available in Firefox are also used so that errors in the input are highlighted in the learners' text box, allowing correction of the text before submission. Given the complex orthography of Irish this ensures that the users' spelling errors don't result in a breakdown of the communication.

At the present stage of development 11 topics (aligned to the second level oral examination curriculum, including 'family', 'holidays', 'hobbies', etc.) consisting of 3,670 categories have been added in order to make *Taidhgín* seem 'intelligent' (category = a conversational turn consisting of a question with potentially multiple responses, including anticipated errors, as discussed above).

Early elements of grammar and spelling correction facilities have been included in the prototype design to date. The example in Figure 2 illustrates one example, i.e. the numerical system in Irish, which is relatively complex. The learner's error and *Taidhgín*'s corrected versions are shown in boldface. The number '2', for example, can be expressed as *dó, dhá, beirt, dara, dóú / dhó* depending on the context in which it arises. For example, the terms *dhá* and *beirt* are identically used but qualify different types of nouns: *dhá* is used for inanimate objects (e.g. *dhá chupán* 'two cups') while *beirt* is used for humans (e.g. *beirt chailín* 'two girls'). Both correct and incorrect usages are anticipated in the preparation of the categories for

Taidhgín. If the learner used ******dhá* *deartháir* *'two brothers' instead of **beirt** *deartháir* 'two brothers' the correct version is recast by *Taidhgín* and the conversation continues.

Another area with which learners tend to have trouble concerns the two forms of the verb '**to be**' in Irish. The copula *is* exhibits a characteristic of permanency and stability, and is used to express nationality or profession, for example, *Is múinteoir mé* ➔ 'I **am** a teacher'. The substantive verb *bí* (*tá / níl* 'I am / I am not') is employed to describe a more transitory state (*Tá mé ag obair* ➔ 'I **am** working'). Again, in the AIML categories common errors that learners make were predicted and hardcoded so that the system could provide corrective feedback as appropriate.

4 Next steps towards incorporation of 'intelligence'

In its current implementation, *Taidhgín* is faking it. He is not intelligent in the sense of being able to identify an error and correct it: rather, he simply has hardcoded error versions for very specific sentences pertaining to the topics developed so far. Our vision for the future is to give *Taidhgín* more of a brain, so, rather than merely pattern matching, the system can access correct/incorrect usage of grammatical rules, etc. and formulate correct versions.

As part of a Digital Plan for Irish Speech and Language Technology (2016 - 2026), commissioned by the Department of Arts, Heritage Regional, Rural and Gaeltacht Affairs, NLP and speech technology resources are being developed for Irish and we look to some of these developments to grow *Taidhgín*'s intelligence. Resources that are already available include a grammar checking engine, (Scannell, 2005), available in Firefox and usable with *Taidhgín*, a morphological analyser (Uí Dhonnchadha, Nic Pháidín, & Van Genabith, 2003), a part-of-speech tagger (Uí Dhonnchadha & Van Genabith, 2006), and a chunker (Uí Dhonnchadha & Van Genabith, 2010).

A recently developed resource is the semantic WordNet for Irish (O'Regan, Scannell, & Uí Dhonnchadha, 2016) which classifies lexical units into categories, e.g. *profession* or *nationality*. If *Taidhgín* can detect such information in the learner's input it should enable him to spot whether the correct form of the verb 'to be' is being used, i.e. the copula *is* or the substantive verb *bí*. This is a simple case where error detection can be generalised rather than being dependent on hardcoding.

Corrective feedback for the learner can be presented either implicitly (where the correction is recast by the dialogue partner and flow is not interrupted) as illustrated in Figure 2, or explicitly (more on this below).

As with the forms of the verb 'to be', animate and inanimate nouns can be classified in WordNet and this can be used to identify correct/incorrect usage of the numerals, as discussed above (see also Figure 2).

The use of NLP tools will serve different purposes in making *Taidhgín* a useful pedagogical aid. For example, the morphological analyser and generator (Uí Dhonnchadha et al., 2003) can be used both for the creation of CALL content (quizzes, etc. for grammatical drilling) and to allow *Taidhgín* to identify if the learner's input violates grammatical rules such as tense and verb conjugation, etc. Similarly, the spelling and grammar checker/corrector (Scannell, 2005) can be used for developing drills as well as ensuring comprehensible learner input to *Taidhgín* so that the system can recognise the learner's string and respond appropriately, ensuring there are fewer breakdowns in communication.

The future plan is to incorporate these new technologies into the *Taidhgín* conversational pedagog-ical agent platform in order to develop a combination of form-focused instruction and meaning-focused conversation.

It is intended that the learner would start by *chatting* to *Taidhgín* and if/when errors should be detected by the system, learners would be given the option either to leave the conversation, focus on form and concentrate on a specific aspect of the language with which they have difficulty (see Figure 3: *Trialacha Taidhgín* 'Exercises with Taidhgín' for options to train certain linguistic features) or to continue with meaning-focused conversation, maximising 'flow' or the engagement of the learner with the task (Csíkszentmihályi, 1988) while the learning process is being steered with the inclusion of appropriately scaffolded material.

Up to now we've talked about how *Taidhgín* might detect errors. It is important to note that there are several remedial approaches that can be taken beyond the implicit recasting and explicit focus on form drilling mentioned above. If errors are logged and it transpires a particular error is made a set number of times, *Taidhgín* could adapt the dialogue so that areas where the learner needs additional practice are foregrounded (implicitly, e.g. if past tense formation is a problem, *Taidhgín* could frame his questions in the past tense).

Alternatively, *Taidhgín* can explicitly draw the learner's attention to the correct form with 'did you mean X?' questions. *Taidhgín* could even prompt the learner to leave the guided free dialogue and spend some time instead practicing using a fun, contextualised exercise designed specifically to drill a particular linguistic feature of Irish. The interface to such drills is illustrated in Figure 3.

Personal profiles will be constructed for individual language learners so that the responses by the avatar may be more finely tuned to the individual. This not only helps a more adaptive learning environment but should enable a degree of personalisation of content in such a way as to engage the learner by having the avatar establish a rapport with them.

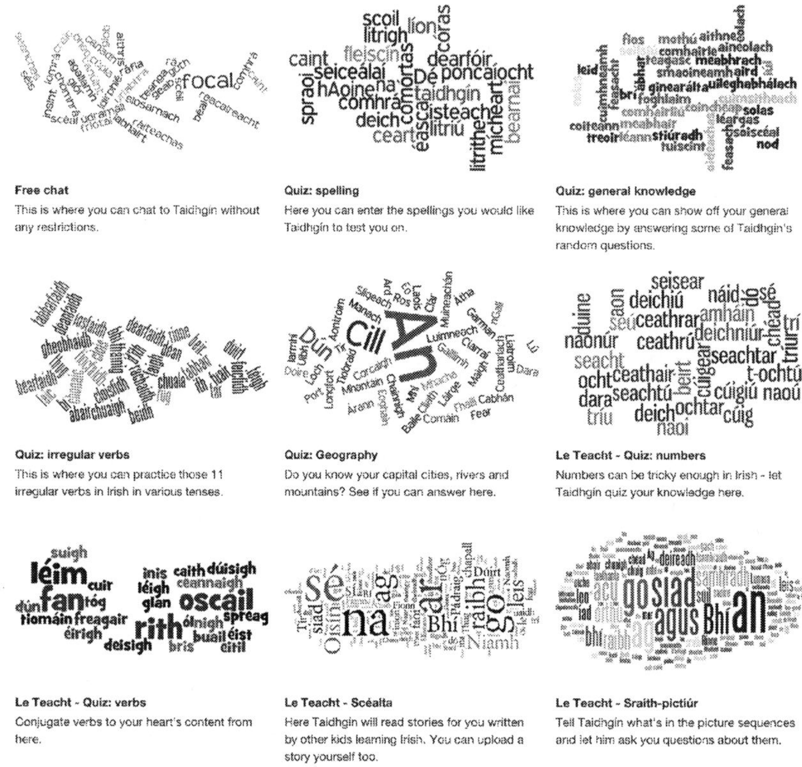

Figure 3: *Trialacha Taidhgín* 'Exercises with *Taidhgín*': interface to a range of focus on form exercises including, for example, quizzes on irregular verbs, spelling, general knowledge, etc

This paper has discussed those aspects of intelligence that we would hope to work towards incorporating into such dialogue systems. Of course there are other aspects of *Taidhgín's* growing brain that will need some attention: he will need to be able to 'hear' what the learner says to him in order to conduct a more meaningful conversation. Within the context of the Digital Plan for Irish (2016-2026), speech recognition is envisaged. Incorporating recognition into *Taidhgín* will enable a full end-to-end spoken dialogue system. A full recognition system will inevitably take time to develop but even a partial system could, in the short-term, provide interesting options. It will be important to ensure that the future spoken output of *Taidhgín* can handle the conversational prosody of true dialogues.

5   Conclusions

The overall goal is to harness the emerging technologies in a way that will enable more effective language learning. It is planned to incorporate more NLP resources as well as speech resources into the current prototype of the *Taidhgín* system which will both ensure that the flow of dialogue is less likely to fail, and also enable the dialogue system to pick up on incorrect forms, respond appropriately to the learner and provide intelligent corrective feedback.

As the simple prototype illustrated above indicates there is great potential for developments in this field. It is hoped that the *Taidhgín* prototype might benefit those dealing with the ever more daunting task of maintaining endangered languages through education. The future survival of Irish and many such endangered languages will depend on how effectively they can be transmitted to the next generation. In this context, there is some urgency with ensuring that our educational resources make full use of what modern speech and language technologies have to offer.

Acknowledgments

The authors gratefully acknowledge funding from the Department of Arts, Heritage, Regional, Rural and Gaeltacht Affairs, Ireland (the ABAIR project) and from An Chomhairle um Oideachas Gaeltachta & Gaelscolaíochta (the CabairE project).

References

Csíkszentmihályi, M. (1988). The flow experience and its significance for human psychology. In M. Csíkszentmihalyi & I. S. Csíkszentmihalyi (Eds.), *Optimal experience: Psychological studies of flow in consciousness* (pp. 15–35). Cambridge: Cambridge University Press.

Eurydice. (2013). *Recommended Annual Taught Time in Full-time Compulsory Education in Europe 2012/13. Eurydice - Facts and Figures, European Commission.* Retrieved from http://eacea.ec.europa.eu/education/eurydice/documents/facts_and_figures/taught_time_EN.pdf

Moseley, C. (Ed.). (2010). *Atlas of the world's languages in danger* (3rd ed.). Paris: UNESCO Publishing. Retrieved from http://www.unesco.org/culture/en/endangeredlanguages/atlas

Ní Chiaráin, N. (2014). *Text-to-Speech Synthesis in Computer-Assisted Language Learning for Irish: Development and Evaluation.* (Unpublished Doctoral thesis, CLCS, Trinity College, Dublin).

Ní Chiaráin, N., & Ní Chasaide, A. (2016). Chatbot Technology with Synthetic Voices in the Acquisition of an Endangered Language: Motivation, Development and Evaluation of a Platform for Irish. In *Proceedings of the Tenth International Conference on Language Resources and Evaluation (LREC 2016). 23-28 May 2016* (pp. 3429-3435). Portorož, Slovenia: European Language Resources Association (ELRA).

O'Regan, J., Scannell, K., & Uí Dhonnchadha, E. (2016). lemonGAWN: WordNet Gaeilge as Linked Data. In *LDL 2016 – 5th Workshop on Linked Data in Linguistics. Managing, Building and Using Linked Language Resources* (pp. 36–40).

Ó Baoill, D. (1981). *Earráidí scríofa Gaeilge. Cuid 3, réamhfhocail agus comhréir : earráidí a tharla in aistí Gaeilge na hArdteistiméireachta, 1975.* Baile Átha Cliath: Institiúd Teangeolaíochta Éireann.

Robichaud, A. (2014). Interview with Noam Chomsky on Education. *Radical Pedagogy, 11*(1). Retrieved from http://www.radicalpedagogy.org/radicalpedagogy.org/Interview_with_Noam_Chomsky_on_Education.html

Scannell, K. (2005). An Gramadóir. Retrieved October 3, 2016, from http://borel.slu.edu/gramadoir/

Uí Dhonnchadha, E., Nic Pháidín, C., & Van Genabith, J. (2003). Design, implementation and evaluation of an inflectional morphology finite state transducer for Irish. *Machine Translation, 18,* 173–193. http://doi.org/10.1007/s10590-004-2480-9

Uí Dhonnchadha, E., & Van Genabith, J. (2006). A part-of-speech tagger for Irish using finite-state morphology and constraint grammar disambiguation. In *5th International Conference on Language Resources and Evaluation (LREC 2006).*

Uí Dhonnchadha, E., & Van Genabith, J. (2010). Partial dependency parsing for Irish. In *7th International Conference on Language Resources and Evaluation (LREC 2010).*

Building a learner corpus for Russian[*]

Ekaterina Rakhilina   Anastasia Vyrenkova   Elmira Mustakimova
National Research University Higher School of Economics
21/4, Staraya Basmannaya Ulitsa, 105066, Moscow, Russia
`erakhilina,avyrenkova,emustakimova@hse.ru`

Alina Ladygina
Eberhard Karls Universität Tübingen
19-23, Wilhelmstrasse,
72074, Tübingen, Germany
`aladygina@yahoo.com`

Ivan Smirnov
Sholokhov Moscow State
University for the Humanities
3/7a Vladimirskaya Ulitsa,
111123, Moscow, Russia
`smirnof.van@gmail.com`

Abstract

In this paper we describe an open learner corpus of Russian. The Russian Learner Corpus (RLC) is the first corpus with clear distinction between foreign language learners and heritage speakers. We discuss the structure of the corpus, its development and the annotation principles. This paper describes the platform of the RLC which combines online tools for text uploading, processing, error annotation and corpus search.

1 Introduction

Designing learner corpora has become a rapidly developing branch of corpus linguistics, which is accounted for by obvious reasons — both research and practical. As annotated collections of texts produced by non-native speakers of a certain language, learner corpora open up new horizons in areas, such as quantitative studies in second language acquisition, contrastive interlanguage analysis (Granger, 1996), etc., and the urge for well-organized error classification and frequency based error analysis can hardly be overestimated for language teaching. Moreover, computerized learner data serve as training and test data sets for various NLP tasks, such as native language identification task (Jarvis and Paquot, 2015),

automatic error detection (Leacock et al., 2014), etc. The goal of this paper is to present a recently created Russian Learner Corpus (RLC)[1]. The novelty of the RLC is threefold:

1. It is the first open learner corpus for the Russian language enabling search over lemma, grammatical features, and error tags;

2. It is the first learner corpus that draws a clear distinction between HL (heritage language)[2] and L2 (second language) speakers;

3. It is built on an integrated multifunctional platform that provides a single interface for uploading, annotating and search.

Russian Learner Corpus is an international project carried out by the Linguistic Laboratory for Corpus Technologies at the Higher School of Economics in close collaboration with experts from more than 10 countries (see "Our partners" at http://www.web-corpora.net/RLC). The corpus currently comprises more than 730000 tokens. 56 per cent of the data is produced by L2 learners of Russian, 44 per cent - by heritage speakers of Russian, who are college/university-age students at the proficiency

[*]Support from the Basic Research Program of the National Research University Higher School of Economics is gratefully acknowledged.

[1]RLC is available at `http://web-corpora.net/RLC`.

[2]Heritage speakers are a special type of bilinguals who grew up in a non-native language environment, but use their native language at home or to communicate with their family (see (Valdés, 2000))

level of intermediate and higher. The first version of the RLC contained only texts from American English-dominant speakers of Russian. The number of dominant languages has by far grown to eight. Three of them are at the moment scarcely presented in the corpus, however, more data on them and two more languages are being prepared for upload. A valuable part of the RLC is a large longitudinal subcorpus of academic writing called RULEC collected by Olessya Kisselev and Anna Alsufieva. All the respondents signed a special consent form and their names are anonymized in the corpus. In the longitudinal RULEC the speakers were assigned fake names so that the user could easily trace the progress of each student. Other respondents are assigned a unique students code.

In Section 2 we give an overview of similar projects developed for the Russian language. Section 3 describes corpus data and metainformation provided to each text. Section 4 presents annotation principles, and Section 5 focuses on characteristics of the corpus platform. In Section 6 we will make some concluding remarks and discuss our future work.

2   Related works

To date there have been several projects focusing on Russian as a target language for learners. Among them are studies based on collections of narratives (Protassova, 2016; Isurin and Ivanova-Sullivan, 2008; Polinsky, 2008), academic writing repositories (e.g. Corpus of Russian Students Texts (Zevakhina and Dzhakupova, 2015), ReBiSlav[3]) and learner translations (Russian Learner Translator Corpus, see (Kutuzov and Kunilovskaya, 2014). Despite their obvious usefulness and prominence, however, none of these projects can be named a full-fledged learner corpus for the reasons that we outline below.

Narrative collections present a huge interest for teachers and linguists studying non-native speech (see (Pavlenko, 2008) for more detail), yet those that are listed above are relatively small, closed and used for specific purposes of a researcher, which in-

evitably entails heterogeneity in annotation principles. The Corpus of Russian Student Texts (CoRST) is an open annotated resource, however, it consists of the samples of academic writing produced by native speakers of Russian, and thus the understanding of the term *learner* for this project is not at all common, as it implies the process of mastering a new register of Russian by native Russian speakers. Translation corpora are traditionally granted a special status primarily because they contain constrained language production and should be particularly designed.

Another important feature of the RLC is that it allows for differentiating between heritage and L2 production. Contrasting heritage speakers and L2 learners has attracted much attention from both pedagogical and theoretical researchers in the recent decades. At the same time learner corpora do not normally incorporate data on heritage production or probably do not make any clear distinction between heritage and L2 texts. There are also several collections solely devoted to Heritage Russian data (Corpus for Heritage Language Variation and Change[4], (Polinsky, 2008). However, to our knowledge, by far there have been no open annotated resources covering both L2 and heritage data.

Thus, the Russian Learner Corpus (RLC) that we wish to present here is the first collection of oral and written texts by Heritage and L2 speakers of Russian integrated under a single interface and annotated according to single principles.

3   Data

The corpus consists of two data subsets: the first subset is composed of texts produced by second language learners of Russian (about 2000 texts), and the second one contains written texts and transcripts of speech by Russian heritage speakers (about 1500 texts). The texts were collected by our colleagues who are teaching Russian as a second or heritage language and/or making their research in SLA and heritage linguistics. The students filled in the form of consent and a sociolinguistic questionnaire. RLC represents the texts of Russian language learners who have 5 different dominant languages (American English, French, Korean, Kazakh, and German,

---

[3]http://www.uni-regensburg.de/
sprache-literatur-kultur/slavistik/
rund-ums-institut/korpora/rebislav

[4]http://projects.chass.utoronto.ca/ngn/
HLVC/U_U_home.php

including Swiss German).

Furthermore, the data from Italian, Serbian, Japanese, Swedish, Norwegian and Dutch students are going to be released soon. The sampling of dominant languages is explained by two reasons: we were initially aiming at presenting typologically different L1 in the sample, and presenting texts coming from both foreign and Post-Soviet countries. Currently, however, there is a bias in the data that is spelled out by its accessibility. The corpus also represents various genres: essays and summaries of the articles on social, cultural, historical, political and ecological topics, abstracts of term-papers, biographical stories, blogs and narratives (cartoon and pictures description).

3.1 Metadata

In order to successfully use a corpus a researcher should be provided with relevant information about the origins and specific features of the data, i.e. metadata. Well-organized metadata enables setting various options for individual subcorpora thus providing efficient search and broader opportunities for data analysis. It also gives a clear picture of overall corpus statistics.

According to Tono (2003), there are three major categories in learner corpora design: (a) language-related criteria (e.g. mode, medium, genre, topic), (b) task-related criteria (e.g. longitudinal vs. cross-sectional; spontaneous vs. prepared), and (c) learner-related criteria (e.g. EFL or ESL, age, gender, mother tongue, overseas experience). This classification served as a starting point for developing metatextual markup for RLC and led us to determining a set of 8 metadata items grouped into 2 categories: author-related and text-related.

Among author-related items are author's unique code, gender, language background (HL vs L2), dominant language, proficiency level and educational type. Proficiency level is ascribed according to the Common European Framework of Reference for Languages (CEFR) and American Council on the Teaching of Foreign Languages (ACTFL). These scales are most commonly used by language teachers in the USA and Europe, and the majority of texts in the corpus are authored by students with the proficiency level thus assessed. For search unification, we have introduced three general tags for

student proficiency ("Beginner", "Intermediate" or "Advanced"), they also allow to specify the level of students attested in line with other principles. Proficiency level is assigned by the teacher against the scale they work with.

The text related data include mode (oral or written), genre, and time limit. The list of genres available for the corpus metadata was developed in collaboration with the teachers of Russian as a Foreign Language from our partner universities and represents the most common tasks that students of Russian complete to train free production skills (listed in Table 1 - 2). A more elaborated system of genres is presented in RULEC. We ask our partners to provide only free production data, however we dont have any exact information on whether students use any reference materials. In some cases the reliance on extra sources can be inferred from the task (cf. paraphrase or book description).

Category	Description
Authors id	
Gender	male vs. female
Language background	L2 learner vs. heritage speaker
Dominant language	American English, French, German (including Swiss German), Korean, Kazakh, Norwegian, Italian, Serbian
Proficiency level	Beginner / Intermediate / Advanced
Scale	CEFR: A1-C2 ACTFL: Beginner Novice - Advanced High
Educational program type	intensive vs. regular course, course for heritage speakers, etc.

Table 1: Author-related metadata

Category	Description
Mode	Written / Oral
Genre	Answers to questions, academic essay, non-academic essay, blog, letter, story, paraphrase, definition, biography, description, summary
Time limit	limited / unlimited

Table 2: Text-related metadata

4   Annotation

The texts in RLC are provided with morphological and error annotation.

Morphological markup is carried out automatically with help of the morphological analyzer MyStem (Segalovich and Titov, 1997). The tag set of 52 morphological labels[5] meets the standard established by Russian National Corpus (ruscorpora.ru). However, morphological ambiguity is not resolved automatically: every ambiguous word is provided with all possible grammatical analyses, so the texts need to be manually disambiguated.

While designing the error annotation scheme for RLC, we took into account annotation schemes used in other learner corpora, such as ICLE (Granger, 1998), Cambridge Learner Corpus (Nicholls, 2003), FALKO (Reznicek et al., 2012) and (Štindlová et al., 2013). Although these tagsets differ in granularity and error categories, it was necessary to compare various approaches. The annotation scheme of the Czech Learner Corpus was particularly relevant for our project, since Czech and Russian, both belonging to Slavic languages, share certain error types, e.g. inflectional and aspectual errors.

Furthermore, we examined error classifications created for Russian which describe common error types in the speech of Russian monolingual children (Tsejtlin, 1982; Rusakova, 2013), Russian first-generation emigrants (Zemskaya, 2001), Russian L2 learners and heritage speakers (Polinsky, 2006; Polinsky, 2010; Ovchinnikova and Pavlova, 2016). Having compared these classifications, we identified common errors, typical for all categories of Russian language learners, and error particularly frequent for heritage speakers and second language learners. Such error types were included in our error tagset. Furthermore, the error taxonomy was discussed with foreign language teachers of Russian and SLA researchers, collaborating with our project, and was additionally refined according to their suggestions.

The resulting error tagset consists of two tag classes: linguistic error classification and target modification taxonomy. According to Tono (2003), at least these two aspects should be included into error annotation scheme. The first group of tags defines an error in terms of linguistic types, e.g. derivational errors, agreement errors etc. Our classification includes broad categories corresponding to different levels of linguistic description, such as spelling, morphological, syntactic, lexical errors and errors in the use of constructions[6]

Each of these classes contains more specific error types. For instance, morphological errors comprise non-word errors, such as incorrect stem alternation, inflectional and derivational errors, as well as incorrect derivation of plural/singular for pluralia and singularia tantum nouns. We tried to avoid inclusion of infrequent error types in our tagset, in order to make it manageable for annotators. Therefore, the errors which do not correspond to more specific error types present in the tagset, are marked with a more general tag (e.g. "Morph" for morphological mistakes, "Syntax" for other syntactic errors etc.)

The target modification tags denote alternations of learner errors comparing to correct target element, such as deletion, insertion, substitution, transposition. These are used only in combination with the linguistic tags. Also, we included an additional tag marking cases of language transfer. As the influence of L1 can occur on different levels (spelling, morphology, syntax, lexical use), this tag should be combined with a linguistic error type, similar to target modification tags.

Along with the tagset, we needed to formulate error annotation principles in order to reduce subjectivity in annotation process and assure reliable inter-annotator agreement. The focus of error annotation in RLC is on severe spelling, grammatical and lexical errors which result in anomalous production. These errors should be corrected with minimal changes of the initial sentence, following the principle of the so-called first target hypothesis (Reznicek et al., 2013; Meurers, 2015). Hence, stylistic, dis-

---

[5]The tags contain information about parts of speech and all grammatical categories of the Russian language: gender, number, case, animacy, aspect, tense, mood, person, transitivity, voice, degree, full/short form.

[6]The term construction is broadly used within the framework of Construction Grammar (see (Fillmore et al., 1988; Goldberg, 1995; Goldberg, 2006; Tomasello, 2003; Ellis, 2013) and others). We understand constructions in a more neutral sense as lexical and grammatical patterns paired with particular meanings, cf. Russian possessive construction *u menya est'* (lit. 'at me is'), which is translated into English as 'I have'

course and pragmatic errors are not taken into account, since correction and annotation of such errors might require deeper interpretation of a learners utterance and this might lead to high variation in annotators decisions.

4.1 Inter-annotator agreement experiment

The error annotation is performed by students of linguistics and supervised by our team. Currently, the RLC annotation tool does not allow two annotators to work on the same texts without seeing the annotation decisions of each other. Therefore, we designed an offline inter-annotator agreement experiment in order to evaluate the consistency of annotation and to reveal ambiguous tags and/or inconsistencies in annotation guidelines.

The experiment was conducted on the sample consisted of 50 texts (8547 tokens in total) written by English and German L2 students. The annotation was made in files retrieved from the corpus. These have the following format: every word was presented on a separate line consisting of 6 columns — sentence number in the database, word, number of words in sentence, error tags, error correction, and annotator code.

Each text was annotated by two annotators (6 pairs in total). Before tagging each participant received 5 trial texts which were checked by supervisors. The most common mistakes were discussed with the annotators and outlined in the annotation guidelines. Afterwards the experimental sample was annotated, the tag mismatches were counted and Cohens kappa coefficient (Cohen, 1960) was calculated.

We assume that relatively low agreement (the highest score was obtained for syntactic (0.317) and spelling (0.249) errors, while the lowest coefficient of 0.185 was achieved for errors in constructions) was primarily caused by the lack of more detailed annotation guidelines. Although the current guidelines list the definition of all the tags and illustrate them with corresponding examples, difficult or ambiguous cases have not been outlined yet. Thus, the annotators made typical errors and did not distinguish between close error types, such as lexical errors and errors in constructions or spelling and inflectional errors. Moreover, since the experiment was performed outside the corpus platform, the annotators had to accommodate to a new data format and workflow, which might also serve as a source for inconsistent annotation. Therefore, an extensive annotation training might help to increase the intercoder agreement score.

Having analyzed discrepancies in annotation, we decided to elaborate new annotation guidelines in order to improve the annotator agreement rate. We believe that this will lead to better results in the next session of our inter-annotator agreement experiments.

5 Corpus platform and tools

The corpus platform is a powerful and complex tool which enables various search options for researchers.

5.1 Development

The previous version[7] of the platform included only texts written by American learners of Russian; it also had no integrated annotation tool. Corpus users had only access to search interface and they could not upload their own texts or annotate them. The corpus workflow during that time was extremely time-consuming and ineffective. First, the contributors needed to send the texts to the corpus chief, who then sent these texts to annotators. The latter ran plain texts through morphological analyzer, which transformed them into XML files, and then annotated these XMLs using "Les Crocodiles"[8] annotation software which works only on Windows. In the next stage, the annotated texts were collected by the chief and sent to the database manager, who uploaded the texts to the corpus server and converted them into a special format, required to run the texts through the database indexator. As a result, we decided to automate the routine steps of the workflow and to enable the access to annotation for any OS (Windows, Mac, Linux).

The new platform is powered by Django, a web-framework written in Python programming language. The texts are kept in a MySQL database,

---

[7] The first version of the platform is available at `http://web-corpora.net/RussianLearnerCorpus/search/`

[8] The tool "Les Crocodiles" 2.7. was developed by Timofey Arkhangelsky.

which has dedicated tables for each of the text layers: metadata layer, sentence layer, morphological and error annotation layers. Such structure and the general Django framework allow to automate the majority of text processing. We also solved the OS problem by creating web-application for annotation, i.e. the annotation tool only needs a browser and Internet access and does not depend on the annotator's OS. In the following sections we describe the new features of the corpus.

5.2 Online data management

First of all, corpus users can upload new texts to the system and add metadata (see Figure 1), so each user can contribute their own collections of L2 or heritage texts to the project. When the text is uploaded, it is in the first place automatically processed by MyStem which includes sentence splitting and morphological analysis. Then the text is available for online annotation.

5.3 Annotation tool

The annotation tool is based on open-source JavaScript library Annotator.js[9]. The annotation is performed at three tiers. The first tier represents the original sentence: this is the tier where annotators mark errors. The second tier shows the original sentence with corrected spelling and morphological mistakes. The final corrected version of the sentence - with all syntactic and lexical changes that were added by annotators (see Figure 2) - is displayed by the third tier.

Some words in the first tier are underlined: this is done automatically when the corpus system detects a word which was analyzed by MyStem as "bastard". Such feature was added to help annotators find errors; this is based on the idea that the word which is not present in MyStem dictionaries or does not link to any template is likely to have an error.

To add a new tag, the annotator selects a fragment of text in the first tier and clicks the "Add annotation" button . After that a small dialog window appears, it has three fields: for error tags, for correction and for adding a comment if necessary. The selected fragment might be a word or several consecutive words within one sentence. It is possible to assign

several tags to a single fragment if it contains multiple errors. The annotated spans might intersect: for example, one can annotate one word and then annotate a larger fragment including that word and several others. The comment section is meant to contain information about alternative target hypotheses (in case of competing target hypotheses) and possible sources of errors (e.g. examples of calques).

Each text in the corpus is classified into one of three groups: not annotated texts, annotated texts, and texts that were annotated and checked. The last group includes texts that were first annotated by corpus contributors or students of linguistic departments and later that annotation was reviewed by the corpus staff. Annotators and staff members can change the texts category by clicking corresponding buttons in the annotators workspace: "Mark as annotated" or "Mark as checked". The corpus staff aims at having all texts annotated and checked. As for now, almost 20,000 errors are annotated in about 35% of texts.

5.4 Corpus search

As in many corpora, one can execute search queries online. The corpus search engine allows to search texts for exact quotes or perform lexico-grammatical search: by lemma, part of speech and other grammatical features (like gender, number, voice, tense etc). These search queries can be also expanded with error tags. It is worth mentioning that the errors are searchable as soon as they are tagged in the annotation tool. For example, such queries can be executed in RLC:

- Find all code-switching errors tagged as CS;

- Find all examples of incorrect usage of passive voice;

- Find lemma *ja* – 'I, me' in dative or instrumental case tagged with any mistake;

- Find lemma *ja* – 'I, me' followed by a verb and/or a preposition.

Moreover, it is possible to define subcorpora: texts can be filtered by its mode (oral or written), native language of the author, gender, year of creation, language background of the author or level of proficiency in Russian.

---

[9]Official website of Annotator.js: `http://annotatorjs.org/`.

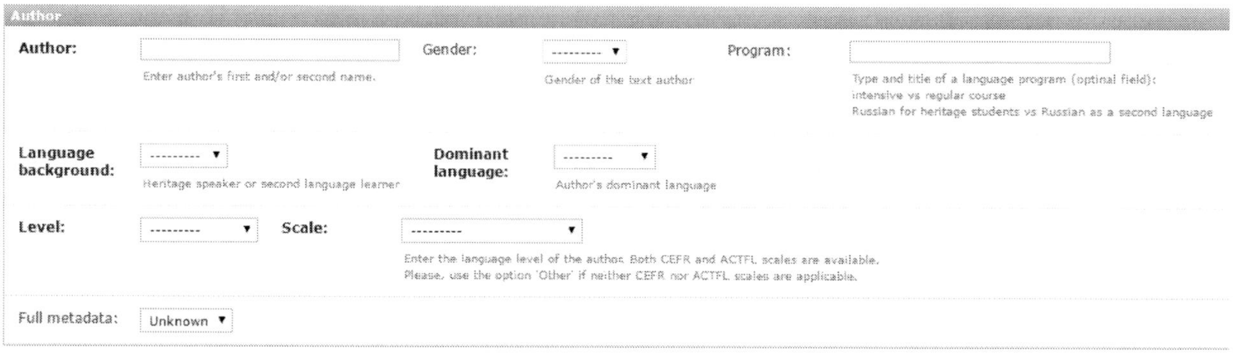

Figure 1: Data upload. Before uploading texts to the corpus, the user fills in metadata fields. The picture shows the form dedicated to author-related data.

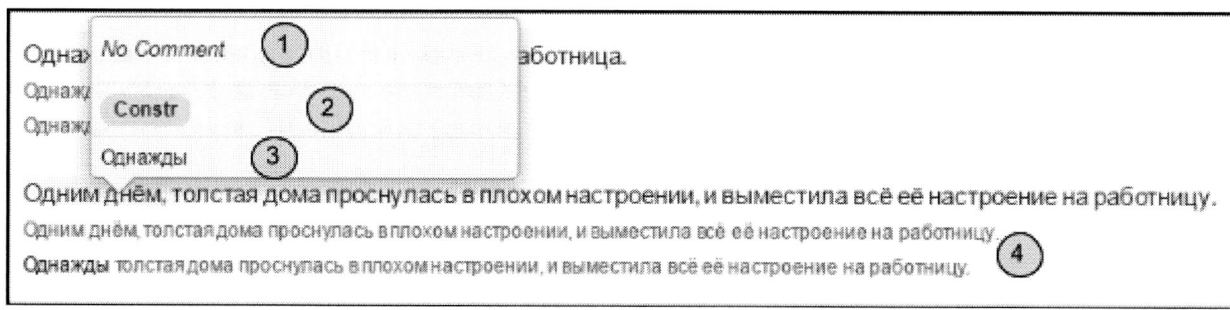

Figure 2: Annotators workplace. (1) Comment field. (2) Field for error tags. (3) Correction field. (4) The two layers of corrections are displayed under the original sentence. All the changes are highlighted.

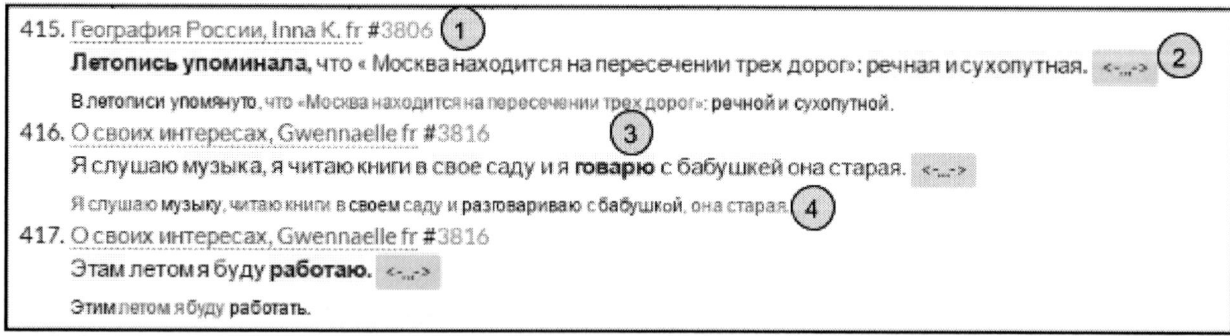

Figure 3: Search results. (1) The text title, author's L1, and the sentence code. The code in only visible to authenticated users. (2) The expand context button. (3) The string matching the search query is shown in bold. The annotations are highlighted. (4) Search results show the original sentence and its final corrected version.

Search results include the number of sentences and number of texts that match the query and the list of all the sentences (Figure 3). Each entry in the results page contains the title of the text, the native language of the author, the original sentence with all allocated annotations and the corrected variant.

There is a possibility to view the context of the passage, but the context is restricted to the maximum of 3 sentences. Authorized users may have more access to the data. The corpus system was developed with user hierarchy, where each group of users has different permissions. Guest access gives permission only for searching the corpus, annotator access permits full text view and annotation. Annotators can also edit or add annotations directly in the search results page and also can view larger context for each result entry. Contributor access licenses not only annotation, but also adding new texts and editing their metadata. At the time of writing, RLC has around 100 users with different access permissions.

The corpus platform also creates a statistics page on the go: it is updated whenever anything is added to the corpus. It allows to see the whole perspective of available data at every moment.

6 Conclusion

In this paper we presented a pioneering Russian Learner Corpus which introduces a clear distinction between HL and L2. This resource has a unique platform with combined tools for corpus search and annotation.

The future development of the RLC is connected with the following tasks. First, we intend to annotate the remaining texts. In order to assure annotation quality, we are planning to improve the annotation guidelines and create an online tool for carrying out inter-annotator agreement experiments. Second, we will add more texts with different L1s and balance dominant languages in the corpus. Third, our team is going to improve the corpus search tool, for example, by including an option to save selected search results to the users directory.

Although not all texts have been annotated yet, the corpus still enables to retrieve interesting patterns in over- and under-using of certain constructions, some of them have been already described in linguistic research (Vyrenkova et al., 2014; Rakhilina, 2015; Polinsky et al., 2016). The annotated corpus data can also have numerous NLP applications, e.g. automatic error correction for language learners, automatic error tagging, author's native language identification. For example, the RLC data served as training and test data for tools for automatic error detection (Klyachko et al., 2013; Ramsajtseva et al., 2016). Therefore, we believe that the further corpus development will open new opportunities for SLA and heritage linguistics research, teaching Russian and creating tools for analyzing Russian learner interlanguage.

Acknowledgments

We would like to express our deep gratitude to everyone who has contributed to the project: Maria Polinsky (University of Maryland), Olessya Kisselev (Penn State University), Anna Alsufieva, Evgeny Dengub (Middlebury Langugage Schools), Irina Dubinina (Brandeis University), Anna Mikhaylova (University of Oregon), Alla Smyslova (Columbia University), Ekaterina Protassova (University of Helsinki), Anna Pavlova (University of Mainz), Anna Möhl (Johannes Gutenberg University of Zurich), Anka Bergmann (Humboldt University of Berlin), Irina Kor Chahine (Aix-Marseille University), Suhyoun Lee (Seoul National University), Svetlana Slavkova, Francesca Biagini and Monica Perotto (Bologna University), Svetlana Sokolova (Tromse University), Natalia Ringblom (University of Stockholm), Hayashida Rie (Osaka University), Margarita Kazakevich (Osaka Universty), Nazija Zhanpeisova (Aktubinsk University), Timofey Arkhangelsky, Olga Eremina, Ekaterina Shnittke and Evgenia Smolovskaya (Higher School of Economics), as well as BA and MA students ("Fundamental and Computational Linguistics" program at the Higher School of Economics) who at different years participated in annotation process.

We would like to thank the anonymous reviewers for their valuable and insightful comments.

References

Jacob Cohen. 1960. A coefficient of agreement for nominal scales. *Educational and Psychological Measurement*, 20(1):37–46.

N. C. Ellis, 2013. *Oxford Handbook of Construction Grammar*, chapter Second language acquisition, pages 365–378. Oxford University Press, Oxford.

Charles J. Fillmore, Paul Kay, and Mary Catherine O'Connor. 1988. Regularity and idiomaticity in grammatical constructions: the case of let alone. *Language*, 64(3):501–538.

Adele Goldberg. 1995. *Constructions: A Construction Grammar Approach to Argument Structure*. University of Chicago Press, Chicago.

Adele Goldberg. 2006. *Constructions at Work: The Nature of Generalization in Grammar*. Oxford University Press, Oxford.

Sylviane Granger. 1996. From CA to CIA and back: An integrated approach to computerized bilingual and learner corpora. *Lund Studies in English*, 88:37–51.

Sylviane. Granger, 1998. *The computer learner corpus: a versatile new source of data for SLA research*, pages 191–202. Longman, London.

Ludmila Isurin and Tanya Ivanova-Sullivan. 2008. Lost in between: The case of Russian heritage speakers. *Heritage Language Journal*, 6(1):72–104.

S. Jarvis and M. Paquot, 2015. *Native language identification*. Cambridge University Press.

Elena Klyachko, Timofey Arkhangelskiy, Olesya Kisselev, and Ekaterina Rakhilina. 2013. Automatic error detection in Russian learner language. In *Proceedings of the First workshop Corpus Analysis with Noise in the Signal (CANS 2013)*, Lancaster, United Kingdom.

Andrey Kutuzov and Maria Kunilovskaya, 2014. *Russian Learner Translator Corpus*, pages 315–323. Springer International Publishing, Cham.

C. Leacock, M. Chodorow, M. Gamon, and J. Tetreault. 2014. *Automated Grammatical Error Detection for Language Learners: Second Edition*. Synthesis Lectures on Human Language Technologies. Morgan & Claypool Publishers.

Detmar Meurers, 2015. *Learner Corpora and Natural Language Processing*. Cambridge University Press.

Diane Nicholls. 2003. The Cambridge learner corpus - error coding and analysis for lexicography and ELT. In Dawn Archer, Paul Rayson, Andrew Wilson, and Tony McEnery, editors, *Proceedings of the Corpus Linguistics 2003 conference*. Lancaster University, UK.

I.G. Ovchinnikova and A.V. Pavlova. 2016. *Perevodcheskij bilingvizm. Po materialam oshibok pis'mennogo perevoda*. FLINTA: Nauka, Moscow.

A. Pavlenko, 2008. *Narrative analysis in the study of bi- and multilingualism*, pages 311–325. Blackwell, Oxford.

Maria Polinsky, Ekaterina Rakhilina, and Anastasia Vyrenkova. 2016. Linguistic creativity in heritage speakers. *Glossa*. In print.

Maria Polinsky. 2006. Incomplete acquisition: American Russian. *Journal of Slavic Linguistics*, pages 191–262.

Maria Polinsky. 2008. Heritage language narratives. *Heritage Language Education: A New Field Emerging*, pages 149–164.

Maria Polinsky. 2010. Russkij jazyk pervogo i vtorogo pokolenija emigrantov, zhivuschix v ssha. *Slavica Helsingiensia*, 40:336–352.

Ekaterina Protassova. 2016. Narrative. frog stories in Russian: 41 transcripts – ages 5, 6, 7, 8, 9, 10, and adult.

E.V. Rakhilina. 2015. Stepeni sravneniya v svete russkoj grammatiki oshibok. *Trudy instituta yazykoznaniya im. V.V. Vinogradova*, 6:310–333.

Olga Ramsajtseva, Aleksandr Ivankov, Robert Zakoyan, and Alina Ladygina. 2016. Morphchecker for non-standard data: a tool for morphological error correction in learner corpora. In print.

Marc Reznicek, Anke Lüdeling, Cedric Krummes, Franziska Schwantuschke, Maik Walter, Karin Schmidt, Hagen Hirschmann, and Torsten Andreas. 2012. Das Falko-Handbuch. Korpusaufbau und Annotationen Version 2.01.

Marc Reznicek, Anke Lüdeling, and Hagen Hirschmann, 2013. *Competing target hypotheses in the Falko corpus: A flexible multi-layer corpus architecture*. Studies in Corpus Linguistics. John Benjamins Publishing Company.

M. Rusakova. 2013. *Elementy antropotsentrichnoj grammatiki russkogo yazyka*. Yazyki slavyanskikh kul'tur, Moscow.

Ilya Segalovich and Vitaly Titov. 1997. Mystem.

Barbora Štindlová, Svatava Škodová, Jirka Hana, and Alexandr Rosen. 2013. A learner corpus of Czech: current state and future directions. In Sylviane Granger, Gaëtanelle Gilquin, and Fanny Meunier, editors, *Twenty Years of Learner Corpus Research: Looking back, Moving ahead. Proceedings of , 15-17 September 2011*, Corpora and Language in Use, Louvain-la-Neuve. Presses Universitaires de Louvain. In print.

Michael Tomasello. 2003. *Constructing a Language: A Usage-Based Theory of Language Acquisition*. Harvard University Press, Harvard.

Y. Tono. 2003. Learner corpora: design, development and applications. In *Proceedings of the 2003 Corpus Linguistics Conference*, pages 800–809.

S.N. Tsejtlin. 1982. *Rechevye oshibki i ikh preduprezhdenie: posobie dlya uchitelej*. Prosveschenie, Moscow.

G. Valdés, 2000. *The teaching of heritage languages: an introduction for Slavic-teaching professionals*, pages 375–403. Slavica, Bloomington.

A.S. Vyrenkova, M.S. Polinsky, and E.V. Rakhilina. 2014. Grammatika oshibok i grammatika konstruktsij: heritage (unasledovannyj) russkij yazyk. *Voprosy yazykoznaniya*, 3:3–19.

E.A. Zemskaya, editor. 2001. *Yazyk russkogo zarubezha: Obschie protsessy i rechevye portrety*. Yazyki slavyanskoj kultury, Moscow.

Natalia Zevakhina and Svetlana Dzhakupova. 2015. Corpus of Russian student texts: design and prospects. In *Proceedings of the 21st International Conference on Computational Linguistics Dialog*, Moscow.

7 Appendix A. Error tagset

Language level	Tag	Definition
Spelling errors	Graph	use of Latin alphabet
	Hyphen	error in use of hyphen
	Space	omission or insertion of space
	Translit	incorrect transliteration of a proper noun
	Ortho	incorrect letter
	Misspell	multiple severe misspellings (in one token)
Morphological errors	Infl	incorrect inflectional ending (which does not belong to a paradigm of a word)
	Deriv	made-up word
	Altern	error in stem alternation
	Num	non-existing number form (e.g. plural for singularia tantum)
	Gender	gender confusion
	Morph	other morphological errors
Syntactic errors	AgrCase	error in case agreement
	AgrGender	error in gender agreement
	AgrNum	error in number agreement
	AgrPers	error in person agreement (between subject and verb)
	AgrPers	incorrect subject for gerund
	Asp	error in verb aspect
	Passive	error in passive
	Tense	inappropriate tense form
	Mode	inappropriate use of verb mode
	Refl	incorrect use of a reflexive verb
	Gov	wrong case
	WO	word-order error
	Ref	pronominal reference error
	Conj	wrong conjunction
	Neg	error in negation
	Aux	incorrect use of auxilaries
	Brev	erroneous use of short-form adjective (or past passive participle)
	Syntax	other syntactic errors
Construction	Constr	Error in construction
Lexical errors	Lex	lexical error
	CS	code-switching
	Par	use of a paronym
	Idiom	error in idiom
Additional tags	Del	omission (of a character, a morpheme or a word)
	Insert	insertion (of a character, a morpheme or a word)
	Subst	substitution (of a character, a morpheme or a word)
	Transp	transposition (of a character, a morpheme or a word)
	Transfer	case of language transfer
	Not-clear	incomprehensible fragment

SweLLex: second language learners' productive vocabulary

Elena Volodina[1]**, Ildikó Pilán**[1]**, Lorena Llozhi**[1]**, Baptiste Degryse**[2]**, Thomas François**[2,3]

[1] University of Gothenburg, Sweden
[2] Université catholique de Louvain, Belgium
[3] FNRS Post-doctoral Researcher
`elena.volodina@svenska.gu.se`

Abstract

This paper presents a new lexical resource for learners of Swedish as a second language, SweLLex, and a know-how behind its creation. We concentrate on L2 learners' *productive* vocabulary, i.e. words that they are actively able to produce, rather than the lexica they comprehend (*receptive* vocabulary). The proposed list covers productive vocabulary used by L2 learners in their essays. Each lexical item on the list is connected to its frequency distribution over the six levels of proficiency defined by the Common European Framework of Reference (CEFR) (Council of Europe, 2001). To make this list a more reliable resource, we experiment with normalizing L2 word-level errors by replacing them with their correct equivalents. SweLLex has been tested in a prototype system for automatic CEFR level classification of essays as well as in a visualization tool aimed at exploring L2 vocabulary contrasting receptive and productive vocabulary usage at different levels of language proficiency.

1 Introduction

The results of the Survey of Adult Competencies (PIAAC, 2013), where literacy as a skill has been assessed among the adult population (16-65 years) has shown that on average Sweden scored among the top 5 countries out of the 23 OECD participants. However, the national Swedish report claims that the difference between the average literacy levels of native (L1) born citizens compared to citizens with an immigrant (L2) background is the largest observed among all participating countries (OECD, 2013, p.6). The low literacy population in Sweden has three times higher risk of being unemployed or reporting poor health. The results of the survey point to an acute need to support immigrants and other low-literacy groups in building stronger language skills as a way of getting jobs and improving their lifestyle (SCB, 2013, p.8).

A way of addressing the needs of immigrants as well as L2 teachers would be to provide an extensive amount of self-study materials for practice. This could be achieved through the development of specific algorithms, but they generally heavily rely on linguistic resources, such as descriptions of vocabulary and grammar scopes per each stage of language development, or (to avoid level-labeling) at least a predefined sequenced presentation of vocabulary and grammar so that automatic generation of learning materials would follow some order of increasing complexity. To do this, as a first step, we need to examine *reading materials* used in L2 courses versus *essays* written during such courses, to study what constitutes L2 learners' lexical and grammatical competence at various levels of proficiency.

Our study has addressed one sub-problem among those outlined above, namely, a descriptive list of productive vocabulary based on a corpus of L2 learner essays. We have combined corpus linguistics methods, computational linguistics methods and empiric analysis to secure a resource that could be used both for L2 research as well as for teaching and assessment purposes. As a preliminary step, we have tested two methods of normalization of L2 word-level errors to see how that would improve the quality of automatic annotation and the quality of the list itself. The resource is not perfect; a number of iterations for its improvement would be needed, complemented with pedagogical experiments. However, this is a pilot study that helps us analyze and improve the methodology, find out its weaknesses and strengths and decide on the paths to take ahead.

The result of the study is a browsable inventory of Swedish L2 productive vocabulary with frequency distributions across CEFR levels. It is possible to browse the resource in parallel with its sister resource for L2 receptive vocabulary, SVALex (François et al., 2016).

Below, we provide a short survey of lexical resources for second language learners (Section 2), present our experiments on normalization (Section 3.2), describe the resulting list (Section 4) and conclude by outlining future perspectives (Section 5).

2 Background

In developing L2 courses as well as designing L2 tests, considerations about which vocabulary to teach or assess are critical. According to the findings within L2 research, to cope with reading comprehension tasks, a learner should understand 95-98% of the text vocabulary (Laufer and Ravenhorst-Kalovski, 2010). But which vocabulary should be taught, and in which order?

Attempts to outline lexical items to concentrate on in L2 context date back to Thorndike (1921). Several approaches have been used since then to identify relevant vocabulary for L2 learners, such as relying on expert intuitions (Allén, 2002), combining statistical insights with expert judgments (Hult et al., 2010), and lately estimating frequencies from corpus-based sources where several variations can be found: domain-specific lists (Coxhead, 2000), general purpose vocabulary (West, 1953), word family frequencies (Coxhead, 2000), and lately sense-based lists (Capel, 2010; Capel, 2012).

Most of the lists above, however, do not reflect the order in which vocabulary should be taught or tested for L2 learners, or at which level. An attempt to cover that need was made in the English Vocabulary Profile (Capel, 2010; Capel, 2012). For Swedish, an effort to list receptive vocabulary useful for L2 learners was made in the European Kelly project

(Kilgarriff et al., 2014) and recently in the SVALex list (François et al., 2016). While Kelly list is based on web-texts whose primary target readers are first language speakers; SVALex is based on the reading comprehension texts used in coursebooks aimed at L2 learners. Both lists, thus, cover receptive vocabulary, i.e. vocabulary that L2 learners can understand when exposed to it while reading or listening. To complement the receptive repertoire with the productive one, we have explored L2 learner essays.

3 Method

3.1 Source corpus

It is natural that any vocabulary list would reflect the corpus it is based on. It is thus important to know what constitutes the source corpus, in our case the SweLL corpus. SweLL (Volodina et al., 2016b) is a corpus consisting of essays written by learners of Swedish as a second language, aged 16 or older. It has been collected at three educational establishments and covers the six CEFR levels: A1 (beginner), A2, B1, B2, C1 and C2 (near-native proficiency). However, C2 is heavily underrepresented. Table 1 summarizes the distribution of essays (and sentences and tokens) across the 6 CEFR levels.

Level	Nr. essays	Nr. sent	Nr. tokens
A1	16	247	2084
A2	83	1727	18349
B1	75	2005	29814
B2	74	1939	32691
C1	89	3409	60455
C2	2	46	694
Total	339	9 373	144 087

Table 1: Number of essays, sentences, and tokens per CEFR level in the SweLL corpus.

The SweLL corpus contains a number of variables associated with the essays, including:

- *learner variables*: age at the moment of writing, gender, mother tongue (L1), education level, duration of the residence stay in Sweden;

- *essay-related information*: assigned CEFR level, setting of writing (exam/classroom/home), access to extra materials (e.g. lexicons, statistics), academic term and date when the essays have been written, essay title, and depending upon the subcorpus - topics (SpIn, TISUS, SW1203), genre (TISUS, SW1203), and grade (TISUS).

Another important characteristics of a corpus that influences a word list derived from it is text topics. In SweLL, the major part of the essays have been annotated for topics, with often several topics assigned to the same essay. The topics are presented in Table 2 in decreasing frequency order.

Topic	Nr essays
health and body care	117
personal identification	97
daily life	60
relations with other people	31
free time, entertainment	19
places	16
arts	15
travel	15
education	9
family and relatives	7
economy	4

Table 2: Number of essays per topic

Since the corpus is rather small, there is a bias towards the dominating topics, something that we intend to overcome in future updates of the list.

3.2 L2 text normalization

Standard corpus annotation follows a number of steps, including tokenization, PoS-tagging, lemmatization and syntactic parsing. A project dealing with learner language requires handling of texts exhibiting a great amount of deviation from standard Swedish. While texts with normative Swedish can be relatively accurately annotated with existing automatic methods, annotating learner language with the same tools is error-prone due to various (and often overlapping) orthographic, morphological, syntactic and other types of errors, e.g.:

- segmentation problems: "jag har två kompisar som hete S och P de är från Afghanistan också jag älskar de för att när jag behöver hjälp de hjälpar gärna mig och jag också hjälpa de."

- misspelling variations: "sommern", "kultor"

- unexpected morphological forms and agreement errors: "Min drömar"

- word order errors: "Jag bara studera 4 ämne i skolan och på fritiden träna jag på gym"

To tackle that problem, an extra step is often added to the annotation process before a standard annotation pipeline is applied, where deviating forms are rewriten to fit into the accepted norms of the language. That step is often referred to as *normalization* (Megyesi et al., 2016; Wisniewski et al., 2013; Dickinson and Ragheb, 2013). Previous error-normalization approaches include, among others, finite state transducers (Antonsen, 2012) and a number of systems, mostly hybrid, created within the CoNLL Shared Task on grammatical error correction for L2 English (Ng et al., 2014).

A more practical reason for our normalization experiments is based on the fact that after the initial collection of raw frequencies for SweLLex, we noticed that there were 4,308 unique tokens which were not assigned a lemma during the linguistic annotation. Figure 1 shows the distribution of non-lemmatized items across all levels of proficiency.

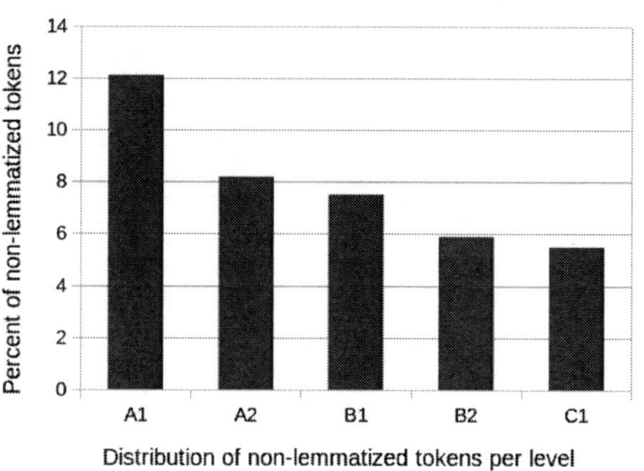

Figure 1: Percent of non-lemmatized items per level, %

We examined a selection of the non-lemmatized words (about 1000 tokens) and split those into five categories. Table 3 shows some examples of the five categories, including correct spelling and English translation where applicable.

Category	Example (correct)	Eng
Misspelling	fotbol (fotboll)	football
Compound	arbetsstress	job stress
Hyphenation	för-söka (försöka)	to attempt
Foreign word	opportunity	
Acronym	fö (för övrigt)	moreover

Table 3: Examples of word entries that failed to match against SALDO morphology lexicon, by category

Level	Correct/total
A1	7/20
A2	13/20
B1	13/20
B2	15/20
C1	16/20

Table 4: Number of correctly returned suggestions per level

To reduce the number of non-lemmatized items, especially in cases of misspellings and hyphenation, we experimented with two normalization approaches at the word level: pure Levenshtein distance, and LanguageTool's output combined with candidate ranking strategies. Our hypothesis has been that normalization should take care of the word-level anomalies of learner language replacing them with a standard variant, so that the automatic annotation in the next step would be more accurate.

Approach 1: Levenshtein distance

As the first strategy for normalization we experimented with pure Levenshtein distance (LD) as implemented in NLTK (Bird, 2006)[1]. LD is a measure for the distance between two strings. In our case, this was the difference between the (possibly) misspelled word and the (probable) target word. Output suggestions were based on SALDO-morphology lexicon (Borin et al., 2013), a full-form lexicon where all inflected forms are listed alongside their base forms and parts of speech. As such, in the cases where the word form was not present in SALDO, we chose the word form in SALDO morphology to which the original word form in our source had the shortest LD, selecting the first suggestion with the shortest edit distance. Suggestions had to start with the same letter, based on the assumption that a misspelled word is likely to start with the same letter as its corresponding correct lemma (Rimrott and Heift, 2005).

Analysis of 20 randomly selected corrections per level has shown that apart from level A1, LD performed quite well at the other levels (see Table 4).

Zooming into the observed cases, we could see that our LD-based algorithm returns the right lemma

in those cases where the edit distance equals 1. Those cases include:

(1) substitution of one misspelled letter, e.g.: ursprang*[2] → ursprung (*origin*);

(2) deletion of an extra letter, e.g.: sekriva* → skriva (*to write*), naman* → namn (*name*);

(3) insertion of one missing letter, i.e. sammanfata* → sammanfatta (*summarize*).

However, when multiple misspellings occur in a word, the performance of LD is rather poor. Also, whenever a word is very short there will likely be many lemmas that have a Levenshtein distance of 1 from the token, and the returned suggestion is often incorrect.

In cases where the first letter is misspelled (e.g. andå* → ändå, *anyway*) our LD-based algorithm fails to return a correct lemma.

Our analysis shows that Levenshtein distance is applicable to normalization of writing at more advanced levels of language proficiency, whereas at the earlier stages it should be complemented by a more complex approach, for example candidate ranking based on word co-occurrence measures as described below.

Approach 2: LanguageTool & candidate ranking

The second type of error normalization was based on LanguageTool[3] (LT) (Naber, 2003), an open-source rule-based proof-reading program available for multiple languages. This tool detects not only spelling, but also some grammatical errors (e.g. inconsistent gender use in inflected forms).

As a first step, we identified errors and a list of one or more correction suggestions, as well as the *context*, i.e. the surrounding tokens for the er-

---

[1] http://www.nltk.org/

[2] An asterisk (*) is added to (potentially erroneous) word forms not found in the SALDO-morphology lexicon.

[3] www.languagetool.org

ror within the same sentence. When more than one correction candidate was available, as an additional step, we made a selection based on *Lexicographers' Mutual Information* (LMI) scores (Kilgarriff et al., 2004). LMI measures the probability of two words co-occurring together in a corpus and it offers the advantage of balancing out the preference of the Mutual Information score for low-frequency words (Bordag, 2008).

The choice of a correction candidate was based on assuming a positive correlation between a correction candidate co-occurring with a context word and that word being the correct version of the learner's intended word. We checked LMI scores for each LT correction candidate and the lemma of each available noun, verb and adjective in the context based on a pre-compiled list of LMI scores. We have created this list using a Korp API (Borin et al., 2012) and a variety of modern Swedish corpora totaling to more than 209 million tokens. Only scores for noun-verb and noun-adjective combinations have been included with a threshold of LMI $\geq$ 50. When available, we select the correction candidate maximizing the sum of all LMI scores for the context words. In the absence of LMI scores for the pairs of correction candidates and context words, the most frequent word form in Swedish Wikipedia texts is chosen as a fallback. Once correction candidates are ranked, each erroneous token identified by LanguageTool is replaced in the essays by the top ranked correction candidate.

In absence of L2 Swedish learner data with error annotations, we performed a small manual evaluation. We checked 114 randomly chosen corrections obtained with the approach described above, out of which 84 were correct, corresponding to 73.68% accuracy. Table 5 shows the amount of corrected tokens per CEFR level. Some of the corrections concerned stylistic features such as inserting a space after punctuation, which was especially common at higher CEFR levels, thus a higher error percentage at B2 and C1 levels is not necessarily an indication of less grammatical texts.

The final variant of SweLLex was derived from a version of the essays normalized with the second approach.

	# tokens	% tokens
A1	204	9.7
A2	1118	6.0
B1	1650	5.5
B2	3526	10.8
C1	7511	12.4

Table 5: Amount of corrected tokens per CEFR level

3.3 Frequency estimation

Each entry in the final list is a base form (lemma) and its part of speech. An entry can also be a multi-word expression (MWE) which is identified during the annotation process by matching potential MWEs to entries in SALDO. Further, each entry is associated with its dispersed frequency in the corpus as a total, frequency at each level of proficiency, as well as for each individual writer ID. Besides, we have connected each writer ID to their mother tongues and have thus a possibility to analyze vocabulary per level and L1.

To estimate frequencies, we used the same formula as for SVALex list (François et al., 2016) to ensure comparability between the two resources aimed at the same language learner group. The frequency formula takes into consideration dispersion of vocabulary items across all learners in the corpus (learner IDs), i.e. it compensates for any influences introduced due to overuse of specific vocabulary by an individual learner (Francis and Kucera, 1982). Dispersion has become a standard approach to frequency estimations, e.g. in projects such as English Vocabulary Profile and FLELex (Capel, 2010; Capel, 2012; François et al., 2016).

4 Description of the resource

The resulting list contains in total 6,965 items. Despite the fact that SweLLex has been generated from a normalized SweLL corpus (Volodina et al., 2016b), about 1490 items could not be lemmatized. In 526 cases it is due to compounds which are not present in SALDO, the rest are the items that haven't been identified by LanguageTools. The statistics below is provided for the rest of the list, i.e. excluding the non-lemmatized items. We compare SweLLex statistics with two other resources, SVALex and English Vocabulary Profile (EVP), to see:

Lev	#items	#new	#MWE	#hapax	Doc.hapax examples	#SVALex	#EVP
A1	398	398	15	0	-	1,157	601
A2	1,327	1,038	82	12	*i kväll* "tonight"	2,432	925
B1	2,380	1,542	206	36	*fylla år* "have birthday"	4,332	1,429
B2	2,396	959	264	58	*fatta beslut* "make a decision"	4,553	1,711
C1	3,566	1,545	430	152	*sätta fingret* "put a finger on sth"	3,160	N/A
C2	145	7	12	1	*i bakhuvudet* "in mind"	N/A	N/A

Table 6: Distribution of SweLLex entries per CEFR level, including the nr. of items, new items, multi-words expressions, and nr. of document hapaxes per level. We also provide the number of new items for SVALex and EVP (Capel (2014)) for comparison

(1) trends between productive lists across two languages, Swedish & English (SweLLex versus EVP)

(2) and productive-receptive relation within the same language (SweLLex versus SVALex).

Table 6 shows that the number of new items per level follows the same pattern as in the English Vocabulary Profile with (almost) comparable numbers at all levels except for B2, where the number of new items in SweLLex is twice as little as in the EVP resource. A hypothetical reason for that could be that we have essays on a very limited number of topics at B2 level (and levels above), which constraints learners from using more varied vocabulary. Since numbers at C1 and C2 levels are not available for EVP, we cannot trace this trend at these levels. However, it would be interesting to see whether the tendency will change once we have collected essays on more varied topics from these levels.

The trend in the receptive resource shows that the number of items increases almost twofold between A1 and A2 in both lists. However, between A2 and B1 students are exposed to many more items than they are able to use actively in writing, at least if we rely on the numbers in SweLLex and SVALex. At B2 we have a low point trend in SweLLex even in comparison to receptive vocabulary, which indirectly supports our previous hypothesis that essays at B2 level have too few topics, influencing (and limiting) the type of vocabulary that students use in their essays. At C2 level we have only 2 essays, which makes the numbers non-representative for analysis.

We can also see that the number of MWEs is growing steadily between levels and can be viewed as one of the most stable (and probably reliable) characteristics of increasing lexical complexity between levels, despite essay topic variation per level.

A document hapax means that the item has been used in one document only in the whole corpus. Document hapaxes are potential candidates for being excluded from central vocabulary at that level. We can, however, see from hapax examples that they can be very good items to keep on the list, covering such words as *tonight, make a decision*, etc. Decisions on how to treat document hapaxes should follow a more pedagogical approach.

A look at the ten most frequent words per level shows that the most frequent word at A1 and A2 levels is the pronoun *jag* (Eng: "I"), which denotes that during the earlier levels, students gradually learn how to talk about their daily lives and people they associate with. This is also apparent from the most used nouns: *skola* (Eng: "school") and *kompis* (Eng: "friend"). At level A2, we see that more pronouns, *han* and *vi* (Eng: "he" and "we"), are included among the top ten words. This indicates that learners are starting to refer to other people more frequently.

At the intermediate levels (B1 and B2), *jag* is no longer the top frequent word, but rather *vara* (Eng: "[to] be"). From this, we can assume that language at these levels becomes more about describing things and probably moves beyond the personal life prevalent at the A levels. Moreover, the verb *ha* (Eng: "have") is introduced among the most frequent words at the B levels. In Swedish, *ha* is also used as an auxiliary verb in order to form perfect tenses. As such, the high frequencies of this word may be because the students are more acquainted with additional tenses.

An interesting addition to note at the C1

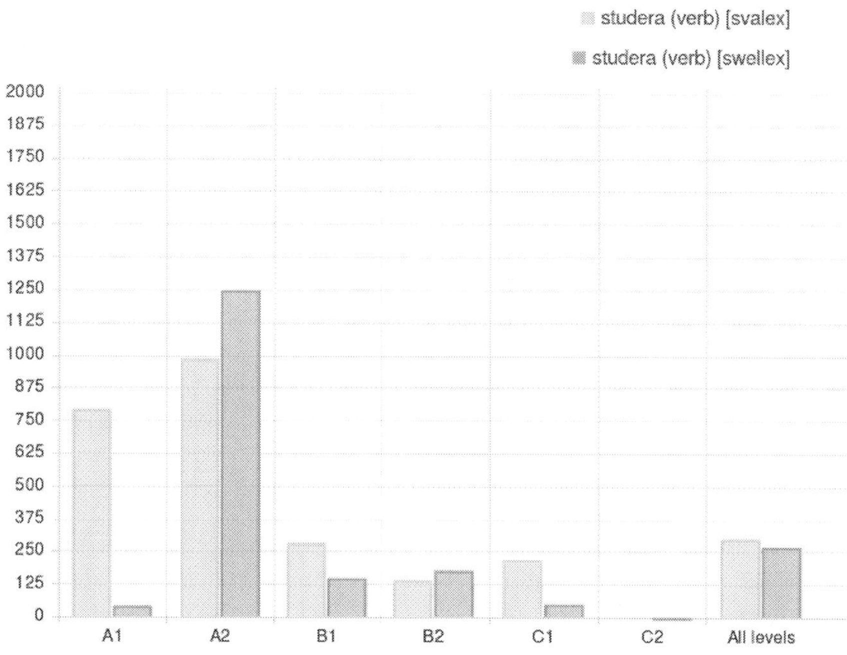

Figure 2: Distribution of the verb *studera*, Eng. "to study", in receptive and productive resources (screen capture from the website)

level is the presence of the lemma *som* (Eng: "who/which/as/that"). This is a clear indication that students have reached a relatively proficient language level, being able to frequently construct subordinate clauses. These are only a few examples of the most frequent words at each level, but they already show the students' language progress. Our list gives a potential to explore further lexical patterns related to vocabulary progress.

Availability of resources of the two kinds - covering receptive and productive vocabulary - makes it possible to contrast receptive and productive distributions. Initially, we matched the two resources to look into the overlaps and possible SweLLex items that are not present SVALex. This yielded the results shown in Table 7.

Resource	#items	#overlaps	#missing
SVALex	15,861	3,591	3,226
SweLLex	6,965	3,591	12,060

Table 7: Comparison between SVALex and SweLLex lists

As we can see, SVALex is an extensive vocabulary list, almost twice the size of SweLLex. Consequently, it is not surprising that 12,060 entries present in SVALex are missing from SweLLex. On the other hand, there are 3,226 entries in SweLLex which are not present in SVALex. Analysis of those items is left for future work, but from the initial inspection, those consist mostly of the non-lemmatized items (e.g. due to learner errors) and compounds.

A more interesting insight can be gained by inspecting distribution profiles of different items. Hypothetically, learners are first exposed to an item through reading, and afterwards start using it productively in writing at a later level. Figure 2 supports this trend. However, words can be expected to show different trends, something that can be explored in the browsable interface for the two resources[4].

---

[4]http://cental.uclouvain.be/svalex/

5   Conclusions

The work presented is only the first step towards a comprehensive description of the productive vocabulary scope used by L2 Swedish learners at different proficiency levels. We have looked into the lexical scope learners demonstrate at various levels productively; two normalization methods at the word level in the context of L2 writing; initial comparison between receptive and productive vocabulary. The method of creating SweLLex needs to be complemented by deeper empiric analysis and pedagogical evaluation; extended by more advanced normalization procedures.

There are multiple directions for future work, including mapping SweLLex distributions to single levels (ongoing work); identifying core versus peripheral vocabulary (must-know vs good-to-know lexical competence); merging SVALex, SweLLex and Kelly-list into a common resource; incorporating SweLLex into real-life applications and tools aimed at L2 learners of Swedish. Another future research direction consists in finding a way to automatically normalize errors stretching over two or more words, as well as at the syntactic level, something that is planned to be addressed within L2 infrastructure efforts (Volodina et al., 2016a).

References

Sture Allén. 2002. *Våra viktiga ord*. Liber, Sweden.

Lene Antonsen. 2012. Improving feedback on L2 misspellings-an FST approach. In *Proceedings of the SLTC 2012 workshop on NLP for CALL; Lund; 25th October; 2012*, number 080, pages 1–10. Linköping University Electronic Press.

Steven Bird. 2006. NLTK: the natural language toolkit. In *Proceedings of the COLING/ACL on Interactive presentation sessions*, pages 69–72. Association for Computational Linguistics.

Stefan Bordag. 2008. A comparison of co-occurrence and similarity measures as simulations of context. In *International Conference on Intelligent Text Processing and Computational Linguistics*, pages 52–63. Springer.

Lars Borin, Markus Forsberg, and Johan Roxendal. 2012. Korp - the corpus infrastructure of Språkbanken. In *LREC*, pages 474–478.

Lars Borin, Markus Forsberg, and Lennart Lönngren. 2013. SALDO: a touch of yin to WordNet's yang.

Language Resources and Evaluation, 47(4):1191–1211.

A. Capel. 2010. A1–B2 vocabulary: insights and issues arising from the English Profile Wordlists project. *English Profile Journal*, 1(1):1–11.

A. Capel. 2012. Completing the English Vocabulary Profile: C1 and C2 vocabulary. *English Profile Journal*, 3:1–14.

Council of Europe. 2001. *Common European Framework of Reference for Languages: Learning, Teaching, Assessment*. Press Syndicate of the University of Cambridge.

Averil Coxhead. 2000. A new academic word list. *TESOL quarterly*, 34(2):213–238.

M. Dickinson and M. Ragheb. 2013. *Annotation for Learner English Guidelines, v. 0.1. Technical report*. Indiana University, Bloomington.

W. Francis and H. Kucera. 1982. *Frequency analysis of English usage*. Houghton Mifflin Company, Boston, MA.

Thomas François, Elena Volodina, Ildikó Pilán, and Anaïs Tack. 2016. SVALex: a CEFR-graded Lexical Resource for Swedish Foreign and Second Language Learners. In *Proceedings of the Tenth International Conference on Language Resources and Evaluation (LREC 2016)*, Paris, France, may.

Ann-Kristin Hult, Sven-Göran Malmgren, and Emma Sköldberg. 2010. Lexin - a report from a recycling lexicographic project in the North. In *Proceedings of the XIV Euralex International Congress (Leeuwarden, 6-10 July 2010)*.

Adam Kilgarriff, Pavel Rychly, Pavel Smrz, and David Tugwell. 2004. Itri-04-08 the Sketch Engine. *Information Technology*, 105:116.

A. Kilgarriff, F. Charalabopoulou, M. Gavrilidou, J. B. Johannessen, S. Khalil, S. J. Kokkinakis, R. Lew, S. Sharoff, R. Vadlapudi, and E. Volodina. 2014. Corpus-based vocabulary lists for language learners for nine languages. *Language resources and evaluation*, 48(1):121 163.

B. Laufer and G.C. Ravenhorst-Kalovski. 2010. Lexical Threshold Revisited: Lexical Text Coverage, Learners' Vocabulary Size and Reading Comprehension. *Reading in a foreign language*, 22(1):15–30.

Beáta Megyesi, Jesper Näsman, and Anne Palmér. 2016. The Uppsala Corpus of Student Writings: Corpus Creation, Annotation, and Analysis. *Proceedings of the Tenth International Conference on Language Resources and Evaluation (LREC 2016)*.

Daniel Naber. 2003. A rule-based style and grammar checker. Master's thesis, Bielefeld University, Bielefeld, Germany.

Hwee Tou Ng, Siew Mei Wu, Ted Briscoe, Christian Hadiwinoto, Raymond Hendy Susanto, and Christopher Bryant, editors. 2014. *Proceedings of the Eighteenth Conference on Computational Natural Language Learning: Shared Task.* Association for Computational Linguistics, Baltimore, Maryland.

OECD. 2013. *OECD Skills Outlook 2013. First Results from the Survey of Adult Skills.*

PIAAC. 2013. *Survey of Adult Skills (PIAAC).*

Anne Rimrott and Trude Heift. 2005. Language learners and generic spell checkers in CALL. *CALICO journal,* pages 17–48.

SCB. 2013. *Tema utbildning, rapport 2013:2, Den internationella undersökningen av vuxnas färdigheter.* Statistiska centralbyrån.

E.L. Thorndike. 1921. *The teacher's word book.* Teachers College, Columbia University, New York.

Elena Volodina, Beata Megyesi, Mats Wirén, Lena Granstedt, Julia Prentice, Monica Reichenberg, and Gunlög Sundberg. 2016a. A Friend in Need? Research agenda for electronic Second Language infrastructure. In *Proceedings of SLTC 2016, Umeå, Sweden.*

Elena Volodina, Ildikó Pilán, Ingegerd Enström, Lorena Llozhi, Peter Lundkvist, Gunlög Sundberg, and Monica Sandell. 2016b. SweLL on the rise: Swedish Learner Language corpus for European Reference Level studies. *LREC 2016, Slovenia.*

Ma West. 1953. *A General Service List of English Words.* London: Longman, Green and Co.

Katrin Wisniewski, Karin Schöne, Lionel Nicolas, Chiara Vettori, Adriane Boyd, Detmar Meurers, Andrea Abel, and Jirka Hana. 2013. MERLIN: An online trilingual learner corpus empirically grounding the European reference levels in authentic learner data. In *ICT for Language Learning 2013, Conference Proceedings, Florence, Italy. Libreriauniversitaria. it Edizioni.*